Verses from the Center

Also by Stephen Batchelor

Alone With Others: An Existential Approach to Buddhism

The Faith to Doubt: Glimpses of Buddhist Uncertainty

The Tibet Guide: Central and Western Tibet

The Awakening of the West:
The Encounter of Buddhism and Western Culture

Buddhism Without Beliefs: A Contemporary Guide to Awakening

TRANSLATIONS

A Guide to the Bodhisattva's Way of Life (Shantideva)

Echoes of Voidness (Geshe Rabten)

Song of the Profound View (Geshe Rabten)

The Mind and Its Functions (Geshe Rabten)

Riverhead Books

a member of Penguin Putnam Inc.

New York

2000

Verses from the Center

A Buddhist Vision of the Sublime

Stephen Batchelor

Riverhead Books

a member of

Penguin Putnam Inc.

375 Hudson Street

New York, NY 10014

Library of Congress Cataloging-in-Publication Data

Nagarjuna, 2nd cent.

[Madhyamakakarika. English]

Verses from the center : a Buddhist vision of the sublime /
Stephen Batchelor.

p.   cm.

ISBN 1-57322-162-7

1. Mâdhyamika (Buddhism)—Early works to 1800.   I. Batchelor,
Stephen.   II. Title.

BQ2792.E5 B38   2000   00-021123

294.3'85—dc21

Printed in the United States of America

1   3   5   7   9   10   8   6   4   2

This book is printed on acid-free paper. ∞

Book design by Chris Welch

for Maurice Ash

The dharma taught by buddhas
Hinges on two truths:
Partial truths of the world
And truths which are sublime.
Without knowing how they differ,
You cannot know the deep;
Without relying on conventions,
You cannot disclose the sublime;
Without intuiting the sublime,
You cannot experience freedom.

—Nagarjuna

Contents

Preface

I have written this book in order to elucidate the vision of the great Buddhist teacher Nagarjuna. Although Nagarjuna is arguably the most important figure in Buddhism after the Buddha himself, very little is known about him. All that can be said with any certainty is that he lived at some time around the second century C.E. in India and is the author of a Sanskrit work of 448 verses, divided into twenty-seven chapters, entitled *Verses from the Center* (*Mūlamadhyamakakārikā*). Yet while Nagarjuna continues to be revered today as a founding figure of many living Buddhist traditions, his seminal work is almost entirely ignored.

I have sought to translate *Verses from the Center* in such a way as to make Nagarjuna's insights come alive for anyone concerned with the question of what it means to live a free and awake life today. Instead of regarding the text as a work of Buddhist doctrine or philosophy—as is generally the case in studies of Nagarjuna—I treat it in the spirit of a Zen koan, which provokes intuitions of the sublime by forcibly challenging entrenched opinions about ourselves and the world.

The book begins with *Intuitions of the Sublime*, which locates Nagarjuna's central and much-misunderstood idea of "emptiness" in the wider context of Buddhist, Taoist and Western traditions and offers a contemporary interpretation of Nagarjuna's vision. This introductory essay is followed by a poetic translation of the Tibetan text of *Verses from the Center*. For a more literal, academic translation, the reader is referred to Jay L. Garfield's *The Fundamental Wisdom of the Middle Way: Nāgārjuna's* Mūlamadhyamakakārikā. New York/Oxford: Oxford University Press, 1995.

In writing this book I am indebted to the Sharpham Trust, who have generously supported the project for the past four years. Thanks also to Paul Williams for providing a digital copy of the Tibetan text and promptly answering occasional technical questions on Sanskrit; to Gay Watson for keeping my classical Tibetan in working order; to Selima Hill for encouraging me to write poetry; to Helen Tworkov for unwavering support throughout; to Anne Edelstein for helping the book find its way into the world; to Amy Hertz for enabling the work to reach its final form; and to my wife, Martine, for everything.

Stephen Batchelor
December 1999

Intuitions of the Sublime

1

BEHIND THE GILDED SWAYAMBU STUPA, WHOSE PAINTED eyes gaze over the Nepalese capital of Kathmandu, is a nondescript building with a single shabby room, empty save for a bronze door smeared with vermilion powder. Tibetans believe this door leads to a cave whence a passageway descends to the subterranean lake where the Indian sage Nagarjuna was taken by a species of sub-aquatic serpents called *naga*s to retrieve the Buddha's *Wisdom Discourses*. Through meditating on these forgotten and hidden teachings, Nagarjuna discovered how to tolerate the terrifying and fascinating emptiness that quivers beneath the threshold of common sense.

Nagarjuna returned to terra firma to reveal what he had learned. Today the door of the cave is locked and bolted. Once a year it is opened by a Newari Buddhist priest, who enters to perform religious rites. Rumors abound of yogis suspended in meditation and curious pilgrims who have entered never to return.

In the Thamel Bahal, a rambling, dilapidated temple-cum-school in the center of Kathmandu, some ancient scriptures are preserved. Stored under lock and key in metal trunks and wrapped in endless layers of colored cloth and brocade are four volumes of the Buddha's *Wisdom Discourses*. Each volume consists of around three hundred loose-leaf pages made of a pliant black material on which the Sanskrit text of the discourse is meticulously inscribed in gold ink. According to the priest and elders of this temple, these volumes were retrieved by a Nepalese merchant called Singhasattva from Lake Manasarovar, at the foot of Mount Kailash in western Tibet.

During the course of a trading mission—so the story goes—the boat in which Singhasattva and his companions were traveling went down in a storm on the lake. They were rescued by maidens who took them home to their palace. Avalokiteshvara, the bodhisattva of compassion, appeared to Singhasattva to warn him that the maidens were ogresses who wanted to devour them. To avoid this fate the merchants had to escape without looking back. Only Singhasattva was able to resist one final glance at his cannibalistic lover. The others were killed and eaten.

On returning across the lake, Singhasattva was given the four volumes of scripture by the serpent king of the lake. He learns that they were transcribed by Manjushri, the bodhisattva of wisdom, who had entrusted them to the *naga*s for safekeeping. When Singhasattva returns in triumph to Kathmandu, he is hailed as a saint. Since then the Thamel Bahal has been dedicated to his worship; a statue of him adorns the main shrine.

The priest and elders are unaware of any connection with Nagarjuna. Yet in an unkempt courtyard at the back of the temple is a white stupa, said to have been miraculously transported from the top of the hill behind Swayambu to save pilgrims the trek to the shrine at the peak. The hill is called "Nagarjuna." It is now a nature reserve.

Farther east in the Kathmandu valley, nestled among terraced fields of millet, is a temple called Sankhu, a shrine to the tantric goddess Vajrayogini. All alone in a meadow some distance behind the elegant cluster of buildings is a chipped stone statue of a seated Buddha with a halo of seven snakes. The statue is identified as that of Nagarjuna. The villagers treat it with the casual reverence of those for whom the gods are still familiar, but cannot explain why it is there.

The legends which have proliferated around Nagarjuna for nearly two thousand years remind one of those of Proteus. In Greek mythology, Proteus was an old man of the sea with the gift of prophecy. He was an ambiguous prophet, for when people consulted him, he would assume a different shape and elude their grasp. Toward the end of his *Verses from the Center,* Nagarjuna reflects on the relationship between gods and men:

> *If the gods were us,*
> *We would be eternal;*
> *For the gods are unborn in eternity.*
> *Were we other than them,*
> *We would be ephemeral.*
> *Were we different,*
> *We would never connect.*

Although Buddhism traditionally regards the gods as mortal celestials inhabiting a separate, non-human realm of existence, Nagarjuna treats them as the dimension of eternity within the ephemeral human condition. Yet the enduring and fleeting elements of our being are utterly contingent on each other. Neither makes sense without the other. "What," asks Nagarjuna, "can be ephemeral / Without eternity?"

Nagarjuna is a protean, chameleon figure, endlessly transforming himself in response to changing circumstances. Born a brahmin, he became the preeminent poet of emptiness. At different moments in history he has appeared as a monk, a founder of Mahayana Buddhism, the first Madhyamika philosopher, a tantric adept, an alchemist, a Nepalese trader, a minor hill in the Himalayas, a god of the millet crop.

Nagarjuna cannot be confined to any one of these roles, nor can he be imagined as anyone else. His voice echoes through history, speaking in different tongues in different places and times, which are always here and now for someone.

2

If Nagarjuna is the poet of emptiness, then Gautama, the Buddha, was its prophet. For the first five hundred years after his death, the Buddha was remembered as an emptiness. In the fragments of stone friezes that survive from the time, he is represented by an empty seat, a tree with no one beneath it, a pair of footprints, or the wheel of dharma that he set turning. While alive, he referred to himself as the *Tathagata,* the "One Thus Gone." It was not until Greek settlers in India converted to Buddhism shortly before the time of Nagarjuna that Gautama was first personified, in the form of the god Apollo.

As a young man, the Buddha was driven to find a response to the existential questions of birth, sickness, aging and death. This quest culminated in an awakening that revealed to him how human anguish is rooted in confusion and craving. The teachings he gave for the remaining forty years of his life describe in detail a path that avoids the extremes of sensory indulgence and ascetic mortification while engaging every dimension of human life. The central concern of the path is to realize freedom from the confusion and craving that generate anguish. To suggest the way to such sublime freedom, the Buddha spoke of "emptiness."

In reply to the question, "What is liberation of mind through emptiness?," an early Buddhist discourse describes how

> a monk gone to the forest or to the root of a tree or to an empty hut, reflects: "This is empty of a self or what belongs to a self."
> This is liberation of mind through emptiness.

Just as nature or an abandoned dwelling is devoid of human ownership, so experience is intrinsically neither "me" nor "mine." Recognizing mental and physical processes as "empty" of self was, for the Buddha, the way to dispel the confusion that lies at the origin of anguish, for such confusion configures a sense of self as a fixed and opaque thing that feels disconnected from the dynamic, contingent and fluid processes of life. Emptiness does not deny these vital processes. It challenges the insistent fixation about self that obscures them, thus rendering life flat, frustrating and repetitive. Emptiness is a cipher of freedom.

The Buddha describes emptiness as the "abode of a great person." Rather than something to understand, emptiness is a condition in which one aspires to live. Gautama encourages his monks not only to liberate the mind through emptiness in a quiet forest, but also to dwell in emptiness when wandering through villages in search of alms. Living in emptiness is equivalent to following the path to awakening itself. It not only entails letting go of craving and confusion, but cultivating awareness of and insight into the nature of one's self and one's world. Emptiness is a metaphor for authenticity.

The "great person" who abides in emptiness is one who is able to remain centered in the middle way. Although this middle way was introduced by the Buddha as a path that avoids the extremes of indulgence and mortification, it was refined to include the capacity not to succumb to the lure of any form of dualism. The wanderer Vacchagotta, for example, asked the Buddha:

"How is it, Venerable Gautama; does the self exist?" The Buddha remained silent. "Then how is it, Venerable Gautama; does the self not exist?" The Buddha again remained silent.

The wanderer Vacchagotta got up from his seat and went away.

The Buddha turned to his attendant Ananda and said:

"If I had answered, 'the self exists,' that would have encouraged eternalism . . . and if I had answered, 'the self does not exist,' that would have encouraged nihilism."

Although the Buddha taught a doctrine of selflessness, when answering the stranger Vacchagotta he recognized how his own teaching of selflessness placed him on the horns of a dilemma. To be true to his middle way, he had to avoid saying anything that might suggest a person to be endowed with some kind of essential and permanent identity. Yet nor could he suggest the opposite: that a person is a pure illusion, incapable of making moral choices that culminate in acts which bear psychological and social consequences. In steering a middle course between eternalism and nihilism, the Buddha remains suspended between "yes" and "no," "self" and "no self," in silent emptiness.

To dwell in emptiness means living with the ambiguous and non-dualistic nature of life. This is clear from the Buddha's response to the questions of Katyayana:

"Katyayana, everyday experience relies on the duality of 'it is' and 'it is not.' But for one who . . . perceives how the things of the world arise and pass away, for him, there is no 'it is' and no 'it is not.' 'Everything exists' is simply one extreme, Katyayana, and 'nothing exists' is the other extreme. The Tathagata relies on neither of these two extremes; he teaches the dharma as a middle way."

While the middle way is grounded in insight into the emptiness of self, it expands the experience of emptiness into a sensibility that resists any attempt to pin things down to "this" or "that."

3

UNKNOWN TO THE BUDDHA, EMPTINESS WAS ALSO BEING taught in China at the same time by the Taoist sage Lao Tzu. For Lao Tzu, human anguish was resolved by living in harmony with the underlying principle of the "Tao" or "Way." He saw the strife and misery of the world as symptoms of a society in which people had lost touch with the naturalness and spontaneity of the Way.

The fourth chapter of Lao Tzu's *Tao Te Ching (The Way and its Power)* describes the Way as:

. . . an empty vessel
That may be drawn from
Without ever needing to be filled.
It is bottomless; the very progenitor of all things in the world.

The Way is compared to "a bellows / In that it is empty, but gives a supply that never fails." To live in harmony with the source of life requires that the sage emulate the qualities of the Way itself. Like the Tao, he too must be empty of artifice, self-importance and any attempt to impose control on the natural unfolding of things. The practice of the Tao, according to Lao Tzu, does not entail achieving or accumulating anything, but rather "subtracting day by day" until one reaches a state of inactivity whereby "everything can be activated."

One hundred and fifty years later, the Taoist Chuang Tzu recounted the story of Yen Hui, who asks: "What is the fasting of the mind?" He is told:

"Make your will one! Don't listen with your ears, listen with your mind. No, don't listen with your mind, but listen with your spirit. Listening stops with the ears, the mind stops with recognition, but spirit is empty and waits on all things. The Way gathers in emptiness alone. Emptiness is the fasting of the mind."

Yen Hui said, "Before I heard this, I was certain that I was Hui. But now that I have heard it, there is no more Hui. Can this be called emptiness?"

"That's all there is to it."

Chuang Tzu agrees with the Buddha that emptiness entails an absence of a solid self that is realized through contemplative discipline. Yet Chuang Tzu presents emptiness as a playful, anarchic freedom unconstrained by religiosity. "I came at him empty," says another sage in Chuang Tzu's text, "wriggling and turning, not knowing anything about 'who' or 'what,' now dipping and bending, now flowing in waves." Chuang Tzu then tells the story of Lieh Tzu who meets this sage and realizes "that he had never really begun to learn anything." So Lieh Tzu went back home, where he "replaced his wife at the stove, fed the pigs as though he were feeding people, and showed no preferences in the things he did." Chuang Tzu concludes:

Do not be an embodier of fame; do not be a storehouse of schemes; do not be an undertaker of projects; do not be a proprietor of wisdom. Embody to the fullest what has no end and wander where there is no trail. Hold on to all that you have received from Heaven but do not think you have gotten anything. Be empty, that is all.

The Chinese were struck by the similarities between the teachings of the Buddha and those of the Taoist sages. When Buddhism entered China in the second century C.E., it was regarded as another form of Taoism. Many early translators of Buddhist texts had Taoist backgrounds and employed Taoist terminology to render alien Indian ideas into Chinese.

The Taoists believed that after Lao Tzu composed the *Tao Te Ching,* he departed for the West to convert the "barbarians." His travels brought him to India where he became the teacher of the young man who was to become the Buddha. According to some accounts Lao Tzu *was* the Buddha. This doctrine remained a source of controversy between Buddhists and Taoists in China until the Mongolian Buddhist emperor Kublai Khan banned it by decree in 1281.

4

AT THE SAME TIME THAT BUDDHISM BEGAN TO WEAVE ITS way along the silk route through central Asia into China, the dharma was being rearticulated in India by the enigmatic figure of Nagarjuna. Two centuries later, the first known account of Nagarjuna's life was composed from Indian sources by Kumarajiva, the central Asian scholar who translated *Verses from the Center* from Sanskrit into Chinese.

According to Kumarajiva, Nagarjuna was born at the foot of an Arjuna tree to a brahmin family in South India. He excelled in the traditional religious and secular subjects studied by the Indian priestly caste and by the age of twenty was renowned for his learning. But the sensual side of his character was unfulfilled. He and three friends learned from a sorcerer the art of making themselves invisible. They entered the private quarters in the royal palace and seduced the women. When the king learned of this, he ordered his soldiers to occupy the palace. By aiming their swords above the footprints left by the invisible men, the soldiers were able to kill Nagarjuna's three companions. Nagarjuna was spared only by standing close to the king.

The brush with death impressed on the young man how craving leads to anguish. He escaped from the palace and fled to the mountains, where he became a monk and studied the teachings of the Buddha. Within three months he had gained mastery of the early canonical texts, but found that they did not adequately answer his deepest questions. He then met an old monk who introduced him to the doctrines of Mahayana Buddhism.

The Mahayana ("Great Vehicle") was, at the time of Nagarjuna, a newly emerging movement of thought and practice, whose advocates criticized the spiritual detachment and social isolation of those monks who claimed to represent the early Buddhist tradition. Such people, they maintained, placed too great an emphasis on the attainment of their own liberation and ignored the plight of the world. The Mahayanists took as their ideal the bodhisattva: one who seeks awakening not merely for his or her own sake but in order to be able to liberate others from suffering. Followers of this movement believed that such ideas were not new but had been expounded by the historical Buddha. The discourses in which Gautama taught Mahayana doctrines had, however, only been preserved in non-human realms. Now, the Mahayanists believed, the time was ripe for their dissemination on earth.

Nagarjuna was sufficiently inspired by the vision of these teachings that he left his mountain retreat and wandered through India in search of other Mahayana discourses. In the course of his travels, he refined his dialectical skills against Buddhists and non-Buddhists alike. He defeated those who challenged him in debate and became so convinced of his superior understanding that he finally declared, "I have no master." He founded an order based on his own understanding and then devised a rule for his disciples to follow. It was at this point that a *naga* had compassion for him and guided him to the bed of a lake where the Mahayana *Wisdom Discourses* entrusted to the *naga*s by the Buddha were stored.

The *Wisdom Discourses* (*Prajnaparamita Sutras*) are a series of inspirational dialogues between the Buddha and his leading disciples, and explore at length the metaphysical implications of emptiness. Through studying these texts Nagarjuna was convinced of the centrality of emptiness in the process of awakening. For he realized that the path taught by the Buddha was grounded in a deep, intuitive understanding of the sublime contingency of self and things. On returning to India from the *naga* realms, he then composed *Verses from the Center* and other commentaries on the *Wisdom Discourses,* thus accelerating the spread of Mahayana Buddhism.

A story is told in which Nagarjuna's renown became such that he was invited by a king to participate in a contest of magical powers with a brahmin scholar. The brahmin created a lake, seated himself on a giant lotus flower in the center of it and mocked Nagarjuna for being stranded on solid ground like an ox. In response, Nagarjuna conjured up a white elephant that crushed the lotus seat and tossed the brahmin back onto dry land. The brahmin admitted defeat but made a wish that Nagarjuna were dead. Nagarjuna locked himself inside a room. The next day a worried disciple broke down the door. A cicada flew out. The room was empty.

Kumarajiva's biography appears to weave two entirely different versions of Nagarjuna's life into a single narrative. The first version depicts Nagarjuna as a passionate trickster figure with an exceptional critical intelligence, unwilling to compromise his own search for truth by settling for the dogmas of either Brahmanism or Buddhism. This version, which imputes to Nagarjuna an intention to found his own order and rule, rings true because it is hard to see what sectarian interests would have been served by adding this detail later.

While nothing can be inferred from Nagarjuna's *Verses from the Center* about his early life, the dedication and other passages show that Nagarjuna had a deep faith in the historical Buddha, Gautama. The text also confirms his familiarity with the early Buddhist tradition: the only discourse of the Buddha mentioned by name is the *Questions of Katyayana,* a text preserved in the Pali Canon. Nagarjuna also refers to at least one early Mahayana discourse, the *Questions of Kashyapa.* Throughout *Verses from the Center* one is impressed by the workings of a highly developed analytical intelligence, consonant with the claim that he was a brilliant dialectician.

The second version of Nagarjuna's life, however, is not only less historically plausible but reveals through its overlay of mythical elements how Nagarjuna came to be represented as a founder of Mahayana Buddhism. Yet nowhere in *Verses from the Center* is there a reference to either the Buddha's *Wisdom Discourses* or the Mahayana ideal of the bodhisattva. Not only does Nagarjuna fail to mention the bodhisattva, he explicitly understands the Buddhist path to be the way of the liberated sage (*arhat*). Since the Buddha compared this sage to a *naga*, it could be that Nagarjuna received teachings on emptiness that had been preserved as an oral tradition in the early schools.

Whatever the case, Nagarjuna is convinced that the intelligence which animates the Buddhist path is incompatible with any orthodoxy. He concludes his inquiry into the self with these lines:

> *When buddhas don't appear*
> *And their followers are gone,*
> *The wisdom of awakening*
> *Bursts forth by itself.*

If Nagarjuna considered the vitality of the early tradition to be exhausted and the Mahayana as propounded through the *Wisdom Discourses* to be the way forward, why did he not use this verse as an opportune moment to extol the virtues of the bodhisattva? Instead he looks to the emergence of "solitary buddhas" (*pratyekabuddha*): those who achieve awakening independently of Buddhist institutions through their own insight into contingency and emptiness.

Whoever else he may have been, Nagarjuna was indisputably the first person after the historical Buddha to disclose the dharma in a voice of his own. Until then, Buddhists had confined themselves to remembering the discourses given by Gautama, while classifying, defining and cross-referencing his key terms and ideas into encyclopedic (*abhidharma*) and metaphysical systems. By the time of Nagarjuna, there was no consensus among different Buddhist schools either as to what constituted an authoritative canon, or to what the welter of conflicting discourses meant.

In this uncertain milieu, Nagarjuna's *Verses from the Center* served as a catalyst to trigger the chain of events that was to revolutionize Buddhist tradition. Through his startling sequence of verses, Nagarjuna recovered the core liberating insights of the Buddha's teaching and articulated them in an original and compelling language. He opened up the possibility of tradition being animated as much by contemporary voices as by reference to ancient discourses and encyclopedias.

The key to Nagarjuna's *Verses from the Center* lies in his understanding of emptiness as inseparable from the utter contingency of life itself. Moreover, the emptiness experienced by easing one's obsessive hold on a fixed self or on things is declared by Nagarjuna to be the Buddha's middle way:

Contingency is emptiness
Which, contingently configured,
Is the middle way.

Emptiness is not a *state* but a *way*. Not only is it insepara-
ble from the world of contingencies, it too is "contin-
gently configured." To experience emptiness is not a
descent into an abyss of nothingness nor an ascent into a
separate realm. It is a recovery of the freedom to config-
ure oneself as an intentional, unimpeded trajectory
through the shifting, ambiguous sands of life. To recognize
this emptiness is not a negation of life: it gives us a glimpse
of what enables anything to happen at all.

When emptiness is possible,
Everything is possible;
Were emptiness impossible,
Nothing would be possible.

Emptiness is a way of talking about the sublime depth,
mystery and contingency that are revealed as one probes
beneath the surface of anything that seems to exist in self-
sufficient isolation. Emptiness is the untraceability of any
such isolated thing. Yet for something to be empty does
not imply that there is nothing there at all. "Were there a
trace of something," says Nagarjuna,

> *There would be a trace of emptiness.*
> *Were there no trace of anything,*
> *There would be no trace of emptiness.*

To understand emptiness does not mean that "emptiness" becomes a discrete "object" of a "consciousness." Emptiness is experienced as the letting go of fixed ideas about oneself and the world:

> *Buddhas say emptiness*
> *Is relinquishing opinions.*
> *Believers in emptiness*
> *Are incurable.*

One can become fixated on emptiness as easily as on anything else. In doing so, what is intended to stop fixations becomes an insidious form of entrapment. To symbolize this, Nagarjuna compares emptiness to a poisonous snake: a dangerous but fascinating creature that elegantly negotiates the trickiest terrain. While a handler knows exactly how to pick it up, one who does not will be bitten and killed.

Running through the verses is an urgency that reveals Nagarjuna's determination to ease the existential and linguistic fixations that keep one locked in repetitive cycles of anguish. He pulls the comfortable rug of common sense from beneath one's feet, short-circuiting the habits of the mind, leaving nothing to hold on to. Instead of offering the consolations of belief, he holds out the tantalizing possibility of freedom.

Nagarjuna is not interested in simply reiterating the Buddha's discourses or offering formulaic reinterpretations of orthodox doctrines. He acknowledges his debt to tradition while speaking in a voice that departs from its stylistic conventions. A playful and provocative tone runs through his text. The verses embody the movement of a supple but disquieting intelligence, which constantly has to sidestep the logical traps of the language Nagarjuna cannot help but use. His awareness of the contingency of "self" and "other," "something" and "nothing," is expressed in a voice that is quixotic and inquisitive, dramatic and tentative, always poised to surprise:

> *Believers believe in buddhas*
> *Who vanish in nirvana.*
> *Don't imagine empty buddhas*
> *Vanishing or not.*

Nagarjuna has relatively little to say *about* emptiness. Each poem is an attempt to *disclose* emptiness through the play of language; poetry works not by describing its subject with detached objectivity from without, but by imaginatively entering its subject so as to disclose it from within. As a poet, Nagarjuna gives voice to the freedom of emptiness *from within.* He is not interested in confirming what is safe and familiar, but in exploring what is unsettling and strange; the letting-go of fixed opinions about oneself and the world can be both frightening and compelling. Although such emptiness may seem an intolerable affront to one's sense of identity and security, it may simultaneously be felt as an irresistible lure into a life that is awesome and mysterious.

5

KUMARAJIVA COMPLETED HIS TRANSLATION OF *VERSES from the Center* from Sanskrit into Chinese in 409. He also produced two other works attributed to Nagarjuna. These three texts formed the basis of the Three Treatise (*Sanlun*) School, which inaugurated a Mahayana Buddhist wisdom tradition in China. Many of the Chinese who were drawn to this school, including Kumarajiva's chief disciple Seng-chao, were Taoists who saw Nagarjuna's work as an extension of the writings of Lao Tzu and Chuang Tzu. Over time, though, the Three Treatise School distanced itself from Taoism and became absorbed in the intricacies of Buddhist metaphysics. Isolation from the indigenous cultural milieu of China led to its decline and eventual disappearance in the ninth century.

In contrast, the survival of Ch'an (Zen) Buddhism in China was in part due to its maintaining a Taoist sensibility through its anecdotal style, celebration of spontaneity and naturalness, and commitment to indigenous traditions of the arts. Through seeing itself as a transmission "outside of scriptures," entailing a "direct pointing to the human heart," Ch'an emphasized emptiness as a living experience. Nagarjuna is recognized as the thirteenth patriarch of the school.

When the twenty-eighth patriarch, the Indian monk Bodhidharma, arrived in China in the early part of the sixth century, he is said to have visited the court of Emperor Wu of Liang. Little is known of this ruler, but he is portrayed as a devout Buddhist, intent on gaining merit through good works. Bodhidharma sought to turn the emperor's attention away from a concern with spiritual success to an understanding of emptiness:

> Emperor Wu of Liang asked the great master Bodhidharma, "What is the highest meaning of the holy truths?" Bodhidharma said, "Unholy emptiness." The emperor said, "Who is facing me?" Bodhidharma replied, "I don't know."

The Buddha's "holy truths" of understanding anguish, letting go of craving, realizing cessation and cultivating a path are not things in which to believe so much as injunctions on which to act. As soon as they are elevated to the status of icons, they can be as much an obstacle as anything else. Bodhidharma subverts the emperor's religious piety, leaving him with nowhere to stand and nothing to grasp. His provocative reply is a challenge to let go of consoling beliefs and dwell in the unknowing perplexity of emptiness.

Bodhidharma then went to Mount Sung, where he spent nine years staring at the wall of a cave. During this time he attracted students who were as intent on attaining enlightenment as Emperor Wu was on gaining merit. One winter a monk called Hui-k'o approached the cave, stood outside in the snow, cut off his arm as an act of devotion, and cried: "Your disciple's mind is not yet at peace! I beg you, Master, give it rest!" Bodhidharma said: "Bring your mind to me and I will put it to rest." Hui-k'o replied: "I have searched for the mind but have never been able to find it." "There," said Bodhidharma, "I have put it to rest for you."

Hui-k'o's inquiry into the nature of mind led him neither to a metaphysical essence nor to a blank nothingness. He simply didn't find anything he could point to and say, "There is the essence of the mind." The story illustrates a therapeutic strategy of questioning that aims at freeing one from fixations on both "things" and "nothings." Rather than encouraging his disciple to realize "emptiness," which could all too easily have been construed as either something sacred or simply nothing at all, Bodhidharma asks him to investigate the nature of his own immediate experience. This led to an easing of Hui-k'o's vision, in which the constrictive hold of fixation was, for a moment at least, relaxed.

Bodhidharma is remembered for having introduced Ch'an Buddhism into China. Hui-k'o is regarded as his successor. Four generations later, with the teachings of its sixth Chinese patriarch, Hui-neng, Ch'an emerged out of relative obscurity to become one of the most influential Buddhist movements in East Asia.

As a young man, Hui-neng is said to have experienced awakening on hearing a passage from the *Diamond Cutter* (one of the *Wisdom Discourses*), which contained the phrase "where the mind has nowhere to rest." He later described such non-resting as "the original nature of man." For Hui-neng, the practice of meditation entails seeing this nature without confusion. Emptiness is a way of living in the rich and complex world rather than becoming absorbed in a mystical state. Hui-neng says

Do not sit with a mind fixed on emptiness. If you
do, you will fall into a neutral kind of emptiness.

Emptiness includes the sun, moon, stars and planets, the great earth, mountains and rivers, all trees and grasses, bad men and good men, bad things and good things, heaven and hell; they are all in the midst of emptiness.

A more explicit warning against mystical abstraction is illustrated by this exchange between Shih-kung and Hsi-t'ang, disciples of Ma-tsu, the second-generation successor of Hui-neng:

SHIH-KUNG: Can you grasp emptiness?

HSI-T'ANG: Yes.

SHIH-KUNG: How do you do it?

Hsi-t'ang closed his hand around the empty space between them.

SHIH-KUNG: You don't know how to grasp emptiness.

HSI-T'ANG: How do you do it, then?

Shih-kung grabbed Hsi-t'ang's nose and pulled it.

HSI-T'ANG: Ow! You're going to pull off my nose!

SHIH-KUNG: That is the only way to grasp emptiness.

This dialogue is quoted by Dogen, the thirteenth-century Japanese Zen master, whose writings return again and again to the creativity, sensuality and immediacy of emptiness. For Dogen, all things "play in emptiness." Every moment of sitting meditation is "like a hammer striking emptiness" whose "exquisite peal permeates everywhere." Nowhere is emptiness more apparent than in nature herself:

> You must surely know emptiness is a perfect grass. This emptiness is bound to bloom, like hundreds of grasses blossoming. . . . Seeing a dazzling variety of the flowers of emptiness, we surmise an infinity of the fruits of emptiness. We observe the bloom and fall of the flowers of emptiness and learn the spring and autumn of them.

The awareness of nature as a field of emptiness is, for Dogen, the culmination of a sustained reflection which begins with an analysis of oneself. Although one's sense of "I" may instinctively appear as standing in isolated opposition to the natural world, meditative inquiry erodes this fixated assumption of self-centeredness. Just as Hui-ko could not find an irreducible essence of mind, so there is nothing within one's body, feelings, thoughts, or even consciousness to which one can point and say, "That is the irreducible essence of me." At the same time, a sense of self is impossible *without* physical sensations, emotions, perceptions, thoughts, and consciousness. Experiencing this paradoxical nature of self results in a loss of alienation that is not self abnegation but a reawakening of a sense of the world in which one is not a stranger but a participant. "To study the Way," says Dogen,

> . . . is to study oneself. To study oneself is to forget oneself. To forget oneself is to be awakened by all things. To be awakened by all things is to let body and mind of self and others fall away. Even the traces of awakening come to an end, and this traceless awakening is continued endlessly.

Whether or not Dogen was familiar with Nagarjuna's *Verses from the Center,* these words are one of the most succinct syntheses of Nagarjuna's vision. And irrespective of whether Nagarjuna saw himself as a patriarch of the Zen tradition, to listen to him as a Zen master helps one hear the provocative and enigmatic nuances of his voice.

6

IN INDIA, NAGARJUNA'S POETIC LEGACY CONTINUES through the eighth-century monk Shantideva, renowned as the author of *A Guide to the Bodhisattva's Way of Life*—a nine-hundred-verse poem that in China was attributed to Nagarjuna himself.

For Shantideva, the bodhisattva's vow to achieve awakening for the sake of all living beings is an inevitable consequence of the sudden irruption of unconditional love (*bodhicitta*) into one's life. He compares such love to "a lightning flash on a dark cloudy night that momentarily illuminates everything" and himself to "a blind man who has found a jewel in a heap of garbage." He recognizes how a monk who follows the Buddha's advice to abide in emptiness is thereby exposed to the possibility of an unpredictable explosion of feeling. For his insight into emptiness does not merely change the way he views the world but also transforms the way he feels about it. His heart is abruptly opened to the anguish of others that far exceeds his own, prompting a spontaneous longing to assuage their suffering. Yet Shantideva retains sufficient ironic self-awareness to acknowledge the irrational nature of this passion to save others. "Was it not crazy," he wonders, "to have made that vow when unaware of even my own limitations?"

To fulfill his vow, Shantideva chooses not to engage directly with the world but to retreat from it. He departs for the solitude of nature in search of "wide open places devoid of any sense of 'mine.'" He wanders freely, resting to meditate "in caves, empty shrines or at the feet of trees." The inspiration of the sublime selflessness of the natural world enables him to see the pettiness of his self-centered fantasies. Yet at the heart of this spacious stillness he discovers that he is not alone but intimately interwoven into a seamless web of sentient life, which he compares to a vast organism:

> *Just as these arms and legs*
> *Are seen as limbs of a body,*
> *Why are embodied creatures*
> *Not seen as limbs of life?*

Just as the hand reaches out to soothe the pain in the foot, why does one not spontaneously respond to the suffering of another in the same way? Shantideva realizes that this is due to a deep, visceral clinging to the idea of being a separate self. As long as one is in thrall to this fixation, spontaneous concern for others will tend to be felt only for those who fall within the range of what is "mine." The pain of those outside this range can then be treated with indifference and even satisfaction.

Shantideva refines Nagarjuna's vision by spelling out the affective and ethical implications of emptiness: emptiness not only eases the cognitive constriction of self-centeredness, it generates feelings of empathy. When

Shantideva dissolved his sense of being a closed cell of self, he did not vanish into an abyss of nothingness. Instead he rediscovered himself as a cell that formed part of the interdependent multicellular organism of existence itself. He realized that his sense of being "Shantideva" was not grounded in an isolated personal essence hidden deep within himself somewhere, but was created out of his myriad and unrepeatable relationships with others.

The emptiness that results from dissolving the seemingly impenetrable barrier between "self" and "other" enables Shantideva to see that "I" is only possible in relation to "you." The very word "I," which so poignantly hints at that elusive sense of what is most irreducibly peculiar to a person, only makes sense as part of a language that includes "you," "him," "her," "us," and "them." There never has been and never can be an "I" existing in isolation. Emptiness is counterintuitive because it contradicts the deepest sense a person has of being "me." Yet, as Shantideva makes clear, emptiness does not eliminate this "me," but transforms it. Contrary to expectation, an empty self turns out to be a relational self.

When the impact of this insight strikes home, Shantideva recognizes that he can no longer live and behave as though the needs of "I" were intrinsically more important than those of "you." For he now understands the equality of self and others to be more than just a worthy moral assumption. It has become an inescapable existential fact. He reflects:

I should dispel the pain of others
Because it hurts like my own
And I should be good to them
Because they feel just as I do.
When both they and I
Are the same in wanting joy
And not desiring pain,
What is so special about me?

Shantideva's experience of emptiness is one that not merely frees him from self-centeredness but simultaneously confirms his initial revelation of love. Emptiness discloses a moral perspective that transcends any notion of "me" deliberately "doing good" for "you." In dissolving such fixed conceptual distinctions, a continuum of feeling is revealed that only conventionally can be segregated into "my" suffering as opposed to "yours." In this way, emptiness becomes the basis for an ethics of spontaneous empathetic responsiveness:

When I act for the sake of others,
No amazement or conceit arises.

Just like feeding myself,
I hope for nothing in return.

A legend that grew up around Shantideva relates that while reciting *A Guide to the Bodhisattva's Way of Life* to an audience of monks, he ascended into the sky and disappeared. This is said to have occurred when he uttered the words:

When neither something nor nothing
Remains to be known,
There is no alternative left
But complete non-referential ease.

By associating this vision of emptiness with Shantideva's miraculous departure from the monastery, the legend suggests a symbolic release from the scholarly and moralistic constraints of monasticism into a life of unfettered ease and freedom. Having delivered his masterpiece, Shantideva shuns renown and seeks anonymity. Later fragments of biography tell of his employment as a palace guard, his departure to the mountains as a hermit, his living with a consort in Bengal. Shantideva's abiding in emptiness leads him to the inexorable conclusion that to love the world entails disappearing into its midst to become no one.

Shantideva was not alone at this period in his rejection

of institutional monasticism. A monk rising to preeminence within a monastery only to reject monasticism in favor of a return to the world is a common feature in the lives of the Buddhist tantric adepts (*mahasiddha*) of India. Like the Ch'an masters, their contemporaries in China, the tantric adepts sought to embody the Buddha's teachings in the domain and language of everyday life and immediate experience. Both movements attempted to recover the vitality of a tradition which, while promising freedom, exhibits a curious proclivity to becoming mired in its own rules and dogmas.

Eighty-four such adepts are celebrated, including Shantideva (who appears under the name Bhusuku) and Nagarjuna. Although this Nagarjuna is not the same historical person as the author of *Verses from the Center,* tradition has conflated the two figures. Like Shantideva, the later Nagarjuna is described as a gifted scholar who renounces monastic life. He becomes a wandering beggar and an alchemist who succeeds in producing an elixir of immortality. Like his second-century namesake, he gets involved in the affairs of a king but, rather than transforming himself into a cicada, he dies, decapitated by a blade of grass.

Because he is suspected of being immortal, his head is taken a great distance from his body to prevent any chance of his being resurrected. Legend, however, tells us that with every passing year the head and body will slowly draw nearer to each other until they are reunited and Nagarjuna will live once more.

7

FIVE HUNDRED YEARS LATER, IN THE LATE SPRING OF 1398, the great Tibetan lama Tsongkhapa was meditating in a solitary mountain retreat south of Lhasa. One night he dreamed that he was seated in Tushita, the Pure Land residence of the future Buddha Maitreya, in the presence of Nagarjuna and his followers. The sixth-century Indian scholar Buddhapalita rose from the gathering, walked toward him and placed a Sanskrit text on his head. When Tsongkhapa woke up he turned to the passage he had been reading in Buddhapalita's commentary to Nagarjuna's verse:

> *Were mind and matter me,*
> *I would come and go like them.*
> *If I were something else,*
> *They would say nothing about me.*

At that very moment he experienced a sudden non-conceptual understanding of emptiness. He described the experience as having turned his world upside down. His vision of emptiness was exactly the opposite of what he had imagined until then. In a flood of inspiration, he composed a poetic eulogy to Gautama Buddha entitled *In Praise of Contingency.*

Having identified the author of *Verses from the Center* with his later tantric namesake, Tibetan lamas such as Tsongkhapa believed that Nagarjuna had still been alive in India shortly before Buddhism became the established religion of Tibet in the eighth century. Nagarjuna's six-hundred-year career (made possible by the elixir of immortality) stretched from the composition of *Verses from the Center* via the retrieval of the *Wisdom Discourses* to the writing of seminal tantric commentaries. Although *Verses from the Center* was among the first texts to be translated into Tibetan, from the outset it was subsumed into the Centrist (*Madhyamika*) philosophical tradition as expounded by Chandrakirti and other Indian scholars.

Nine years after his experience of emptiness, Tsongkhapa entered another retreat to compose an extensive commentary to *Verses from the Center.* This erudite and elegant study nonetheless closely follows *Clear Words,* Chandrakirti's verse-by-verse analysis of Nagarjuna's work. Tsongkhapa compares *Verses from the Center* to "the body that serves as the foundation for all Centrist treatises" and at times sheds fresh light on certain passages, but he is always concerned with vindicating the orthodox philosophical interpretations of the text.

Tsongkhapa and his followers sought to define "emptiness" by specifying exactly what is negated when something is said to be "empty." Without such precision, they argued, one would risk using emptiness either to negate too much, thus leading to nihilism, or not enough, thus rendering it ineffective in removing the fixations that keep one trapped in cycles of anguish. That which is negated by emptiness is an instinctive sense of selves and things existing in their own right. From the point of view of common sense, a thing such as a vase appears to stand out vividly on its own, apparently independent of its causal conditions and components, not to mention the various conceptual and linguistic conventions that humans use to identify vases. Tsongkhapa insisted that emptiness was simply the absence of such a sense of "inherent existence." Rather than representing a doorway that opens to a mystical, transcendent sphere hidden beneath the surface of everyday reality, emptiness merely removes the false veneer of inherent existence, thereby enabling a vision of the essential contingency of life.

In order to transform this rational understanding of emptiness into lived experience, Tsongkhapa and his followers turned to the application of a precise meditative technology whose purpose was to turn conceptual knowledge into non-conceptual realization of emptiness. This rational and technical approach to emptiness is epitomized by a work of Tsongkhapa's nephew and disciple Gendun Drup (the First Dalai Lama), which systematically converts each verse of *Verses from the Center* into the form of a logical syllogism. By the time Ngawang Gyatso, the Fifth Dalai Lama, became supreme ruler of Tibet in 1642, Tsongkhapa's Geluk Order had become the state religion and Chandrakirti's Centrism the state philosophy.

One hundred and fifty years later, at the beginning of the nineteenth century, a counter-movement to Geluk orthodoxy began emerging in eastern Tibet. Traditions that had been forgotten or marginalized under the dominance of the Geluk Order began to engage the attention of some of the most gifted lamas of the day. Among these traditions was the practice of Dzogchen ("Great Completion"), a contemplative discipline with parallels to Ch'an/Zen, whose origins went back to the very beginnings of Buddhism in Tibet.

One of the most articulate proponents of Dzogchen at this time was the Geluk monk Shabkar Tsoknyi Rangdrol, who embraced a broad eclectic vision of Buddhism. In 1806 Shabkar retreated to an island in Lake Kokonor, on the remote steppes between Tibet, Mongolia and China, to meditate and write. It was here that he composed what became his most famous work, *The Flight of the Garuda,* a cycle of songs on the practice of Dzogchen.

Dzogchen, like Ch'an, insists that awakening is present

here and now at the very heart of ordinary experience rather than as a distant goal to be attained in the future. The awakened mind of a buddha is nothing other than the pristine awareness animating one's own ordinary mind at every moment. To recognize this pristine awareness requires that it be "pointed out" by a teacher. Shabkar captures this intimate, oral process:

Now come up close and listen. When you look carefully, you do not find the merest speck of real mind you can put your finger on and say "this is it." Not finding anything is an incredible find.

Friends! Mind does not emerge from anything. It is primordially empty; there is nothing there to hold on to. It is not anywhere; it has no shape or color. And in the end nowhere to go. There is no trace of its having been by. Its motions are empty motions and that emptiness is obvious.

. . . Mind's nature is vivid as a flawless piece of crystal: intrinsically empty, naturally radiant, unimpededly responsive. Stripped bare of repetitive error, mind itself is surely and always buddha.

Such instructions undermine habitual perceptions by pointing out the essentially empty, radiant and responsive nature of awareness. Having been introduced to this "vision that cuts free," one relaxes into an uncontrived, open spaciousness which is neither a state of self-conscious meditation nor an inattentive state of distraction. "Having stripped awareness naked," insists Shabkar, "then guard it vividly. This point alone is important."

To protect such pristine awareness entails recognizing and letting go of whatever impedes it. Ultimately, this comes to include spiritual and religious practices as well as more mundane obstructions. As Shabkar says:

When all I do is think about reality
And let awareness undermine itself—
I must stop.

When I let go of fighting, loving, dealing,
Prostrating, circumambulating,
Sacred dance and gesture—
I am alone and helpless.

When I let go of mundane chatter,
Chants and prayers,
Psychic-energetic recitation—
I am silent.

When I let go of muddled mundane thought,
Faith, compassion,

Esoteric practices—
I am thought-free, vivid.

By systematically stripping away any behavior that inhibits the spontaneous play of pristine awareness, one uncovers a freedom that is a dynamic response to each and every circumstance of life. To illustrate this "sublime play of awareness," a Dzogchen master invites one to "the solitude of a mountain peak where you can gaze into the vast expanse of a sky so limpid no trace of cloud or haze can be seen, where pure radiance alone shimmers." Then, "as the first rays of the morning sun strike the peak," you beseech the teacher to reveal the play of awareness. He signals you to still your mind and stare at him. Rattling his hand-drum, he invokes the lamas of the lineage. When your attention is relaxed and free of thoughts, he utters a violent shout and asks: "What is the heart of the matter? What is it? What is it?"

8

To be empty is no longer to be full of oneself. The Buddha encourages abiding in emptiness as a way to realize liberation of the mind. Lao Tzu advises a daily process of subtraction in order that one's life can be filled. Nagarjuna declares that emptiness is the middle way itself. For

Hui-neng, emptiness "includes the sun, moon, stars and planets," while for Dogen "forgetting oneself is to be awakened by all things." For Shantideva, emptiness entails letting go of preoccupation with "self" to find oneself extended into a network of endless relationships with others. Shabkar understands how the mind's emptiness is integral to its radiant, unimpeded responsiveness.

In a completely different context, in 1818 in London—eleven years after Shabkar wrote *The Flight of the Garuda*—the twenty-two-year-old John Keats described Shakespeare as "the least of an egoist that it was possible to be. He was nothing in himself; but he was all that others were, or that they could become." Later the same year, in a letter to a friend, Keats expanded this idea:

> As to the poetical Character itself . . . it is not itself—it has no self—it is everything and nothing—It has no character—it enjoys light and shade; it lives in gusto, be it foul or fair, high or low, rich or poor, mean or elevated—It has as much delight in conceiving an Iago as an Imogen. What shocks the virtuous philosopher, delights the chameleon Poet.

To be empty of a fixed identity allows one to enter fully into the shifting, poignant, beautiful and tragic contin-

gencies of the world. It makes possible an acute aware-
ness of life as a creative process, in which each person is
inextricably involved. Yet despite the subjective intensity
of such a vision, when attention is turned onto the sub-
ject itself, no isolated observer is to be found.

This ability to be empty of self yet filled with world
"which Shakespeare possessed so enormously" was
described by Keats in a letter of December 1817 as "*Neg-
ative Capability,*"

> that is when a man is capable of being in uncertain-
> ties, mysteries, doubts, without any irritable reach-
> ing after fact or reason.

These words describe a Ch'an/Zen practice in which the
meditator settles into a state of perplexity by focusing on
a question such as "What is this?" Far from being a spiri-
tual riddle to which one seeks a suitably enigmatic solu-
tion, such a question is an articulation of the mystery of
life itself. The penetration of this mystery requires that
one not foreclose it by substituting an answer, be it a
metaphysical proposition or a religious belief. One has to
learn how to suspend the habit of reaching for a word or
phrase with which to fill the emptiness opened by the
question. The meditator seeks not a *solution* to this ques-
tion but a living, on-going *response,* which, traditionally, is

often expressed as spontaneous verse, song and poetry. Transposed to a Buddhist context, "negative capability" succinctly captures the tension between the *negative* quality of emptiness which allows the *capability* of creative and empathetic responsiveness.

Keats may have developed the idea of negative capability from his elder contemporary Samuel Taylor Coleridge, a poet whose intellectual brilliance, chaotic private life and drug addiction made him the dark genius of the English Romantic movement. For Coleridge, the creative sensibility consisted in the "suspension of the Act of Comparison, which permits [a] sort of Negative Belief." He illustrated the capability enabled by such suspension with the example of how the water boatman insect makes its way upstream "by alternate pulses of active and passive motion, now resisting the current, and now yielding to it in order to gain further strength and a momentary fulcrum for a further propulsion." This letting go which is simultaneously an engagement unwittingly suggests how one might tread that path, which, in the words of the Buddha, "goes against the stream."

Neither Keats nor Coleridge knew anything about Buddhism, let alone the notion of emptiness, because no information on the subject was available in Europe during their lifetimes. Coleridge was nonetheless struck by the first translations and studies of Indian texts that appeared in the late eighteenth century. In October 1797, around the time he composed his opium-inspired fragment *Kubla Khan,* he wrote to a friend:

> at other times I adopt the Brahman Creed, . . . I should much wish, like the Indian Vishna, to float about along an infinite ocean cradled in the flower of the Lotos, & wake once in a million years for a few minutes—just to know I was going to sleep a million years more.

As with *Kubla Khan,* this intoxicated reverie reveals how Coleridge looked to the distant and barely known Orient as a source of visions that evoked his sense of the sublime.

The Romantic poets sought their primary experience of the sublime, however, in nature. Both Coleridge and Keats undertook long walking tours through inhospitable landscapes that afforded them awestruck glimpses of the power and magnitude of the natural world. While in Germany in 1799, Coleridge described in his journal how he lay awake at night listening to the "thunders and howling of the breaking ice," leading him to reflect on how "there are sounds more sublime than any sight *can* be, more absolutely suspending the power of comparison, and more utterly absorbing the mind's self consciousness, in its total attention to the object working on it."

In contrast to the sensations of pleasure and delight induced by contemplating something beautiful, an experience of the sublime evokes exhilarated feelings of terror and fascination. These opposing forces of fear and attraction cancel each other out, leaving one suspended in a poised rapture wherein the habitual self-preoccupied chatter of the mind is stilled. One is left in silence, incapable of finding words or images to convey the awesome intensity of the moment. Conventional descriptions fail, for one is elevated to the peaks of human experience while simultaneously plumbing its depths. This pristine awareness may last only a few seconds, but it seems to linger in eternity.

The origin of the Buddhist sublime lies not in the awesome power of the natural world but in the tragic excess of human life. According to legend, the Buddha was raised as a prince in the confines of a palace. Having persuaded his father to let him see the world beyond the walls of his home, he encounters a sick person, an old person and a corpse. On each occasion he is overwhelmed by what he sees. In glimpsing the inescapable destiny of all that is born, his narrow self-preoccupation is suspended and he finds himself exposed to what the Chinese would call the "Great Matter of Birth and Death."

This vision of existence is both profoundly disturbing and utterly irresistible for the young man. Although he returns to the palace, he feels, in the words of the poet Ashvaghosa, "like a lion pierced deeply in the heart by a poisoned arrow." One night he slips away and disappears into the forest to pursue the terrible questions he can no longer ignore. His quest culminates six years later in a profound awakening, which leaves him in a stunned silence because his awakening stems from the same inarticulate depth at which his questions were asked. Awakening, like birth and death, is excessive; it exceeds the Buddha's ability to articulate it in words or images. Nagarjuna reflects on how

The Buddha despaired
Of teaching the dharma,
Knowing it hard
To intuit its depths.

To distinguish between the ineffable depths of the Buddha's dharma and its formulation in words and doctrines, Nagarjuna introduces the notion of two truths. He describes the wordless, silent depth as sublime truth, while recognizing that any expression of it can only ever be a partial truth. For Nagarjuna, this distinction between sublime and partial truths is crucial in making sense of what the Buddha taught. For

Without knowing how they differ,
You cannot know the deep;

Without relying on conventions,
You cannot disclose the sublime;
Without intuiting the sublime,
You cannot experience freedom.

Although the Buddha used terms such as "deathless," "time-less" and "unborn" to suggest the sublime, such descriptions are inescapably partial and inadequate. No matter how refined and evocative such formulations may sound, they are simply metaphors drawn from one's knowledge of death, time and birth juxtaposed with one's notion of absence. Even the term "emptiness" is a metaphor taken from one's experience of such things as empty bottles, empty rooms and empty spaces. Nagarjuna is nonetheless aware that without resorting to language, the Buddha could not have communicated his discovery of freedom at all.

While Nagarjuna is conscious of the inadequacy of any word or phrase in denoting the sublime, his own term of choice is "emptiness." The use of such a bleak and uninviting word is perhaps a deliberate ploy to preempt the tendency to picture the sublime as anything. Although later Buddhist philosophers provided exact definitions of emptiness, Nagarjuna's own use of the term throughout *Verses from the Center* is imprecise. He prefers allusive imagery to rational precision, logical games to tightly argued syllogisms, provocative suggestions to clear-cut instructions.

As soon as it is suggested that the sublime is incapable of being adequately represented by words and images, the temptation arises to imagine it as something utterly incommensurable with the mundane unfolding of ordinary life. Nagarjuna emphatically resists this urge to reify emptiness, nirvana or freedom into something transcendent or wholly other:

Life is no different from nirvana,
Nirvana no different than life.
Life's horizons are nirvana's:
The two are exactly the same.

The sublime may be beyond the grasp of concepts or language, but it is only ever encountered deep within the pulsing heart of what is happening here and now.

9

THE STORY OF HOW *VERSES FROM THE CENTER* FOUND ITS way from India via China and Tibet to the West illustrates Nagarjuna's understanding of the contingency of things. Without a series of verses composed nearly two thousand years ago by an enigmatic Indian Buddhist author, the words on this page would not have been written nor would anyone be reading them. The seeds of Nagarjuna's verses have borne and continue to bear fruits, none of which can be said to be identical to Nagarjuna's own words or intentions, nor yet can they be regarded as entirely different. A Nagarjunian account of the destiny of *Verses from the Center* would recognize a continuity between the first tracing of Sanskrit letters onto a palm leaf in ancient India and a digitalized English version that can be downloaded from the Internet, while simultaneously noting the contingent and unpredictable events that link the two together. The Sanskrit and English texts are neither identical nor different; the nature of their relationship cannot be pinned down in terms of a simple "either/or" logic.

Take the term "zero." Until the fifteenth century it was a Spanish word, used to pronounce the Arabic *ciphr* (which also gave us the English "cipher"). When Arabic-speaking Muslims settled in Spain, they brought with them a system of arithmetic that included a symbol for zero. This was to prove indispensable in constructing the mathematics now used in everything from quantum physics to computer programming. The Muslims had discovered the idea in India, the Arabic *ciphr* being their pronunciation of the Sanskrit *shunya,* which from the ninth century at least had been used in India to represent the mathematical notion of zero. *Shunya* means "empty" and was the term Nagarjuna used as the key to understanding what the Buddha taught. Thus *shunya* became *ciphr,* then *ciphr* became *zero.* We can hear the continuity and discontinuity between them.

Or consider the evolution of human beings with sufficiently complex brains, social organization, technology and culture to question our own origins. We apparently come from the sea, from microscopic single-celled organisms, which over four thousand million years evolved into more complex forms of aquatic life, which then emerged from the salty depths to become amphibians, reptiles, insects, birds, and finally mammals, which branched out into myriad forms including that strand among the higher primates which eventually evolved into us. Looking back, we can visualize this bewildering genealogy of life-forms, spun from ever more complex webs of proteins and enzymes, all intimately connected to, contingent upon and flowing into one another. Yet to make sense of it all, we need concepts and images (of "amphibians," "reptiles," "insects," "birds," "mammals"), each with its own neatly delineated borders separating it from the rest.

Herein lies the dilemma Nagarjuna addresses in his verses: how can we make sense of life without literalizing the very concepts we need in order to make sense of life? For Nagarjuna, this is not just a semantic riddle. A sense of life as essentially composed of discrete bits and pieces appears to be embedded in the grammar of the languages we speak. It may lie deeper as an instinctual survival mechanism, or, as Nagarjuna would have believed, as an inborn, delusory tendency that binds us to a repetitive cycle of death and rebirth. To experience life, even for a moment, in a way that is no longer in thrall to such a mechanism or tendency would require a shift of perspective in the core of one's being.

Theories, beliefs and doctrines can provide a conceptual framework for such a shift, but commitment, inquiry, focused awareness and courage are needed to realize it. Nagarjuna's verses are an attempt to disentangle the knots of thought, language and common sense that keep the author trapped within a view of life that, deep down, he knows does not make sense. At times it feels that his struggle with words spins him round in circles, but he moves on, driven by his faith in the possibility of breaking free from the mesmerizing spell of fixations.

Nagarjuna's understanding of contingency does not come from an analysis of history, the etymology of words or evolutionary biology. Living in a traditional society in ancient India, he studies what is close at hand: the plants that grow around him, the fires that flicker in the dark— as well as his own contemplative experience of walking, seeing, desiring, acting, suffering and holding opinions. He questions what it means for these things to be connected, to have a past and a future, to be different, to be identical, to have a cause or a nature, to appear and disappear, to change. He asks what it means for a person to be a self and an other. Whatever insights into contingency he gains, he applies to his understanding of classical Buddhist ideas such as emptiness, awakening and nirvana, which in turn are themselves further analyzed and refined.

10

NAGARJUNA UNDERSTANDS LIFE AS THE SUBLIME UNFOLD-ing of a complex array of conditions, all of which emerge contingently:

Seeds turn into plants that bear fruit.
Motives turn into minds that bear fruit.
Seeds are neither severed from
Nor forever fused with fruits of plants,
Motives are neither severed from
Nor forever fused with fruits of minds.

Causes, whether seeds or motives, appear to be distinct from their effects. Not only can they be separated by long stretches of time, they seem to be different *things:* the acorn that gave birth to the oak is in no way comparable to the great tree that stands where the acorn was planted two hundred years ago. By paying attention to the sprout-ing of an acorn and its transformation into a full-grown tree, we realize there is no point at which the acorn stopped and the oak tree began. Nagarjuna is suspicious of clear-cut "things" such as "seeds" and "plants" as well as language that talks of them as "forever fused with" or "severed from" each other. Mindful awareness of living processes explodes the myth of things (and nothings) to reveal a world that is irreducible to the conceptual and linguistic images we use to describe it.

Seen in this light, each moment of experience emerges from and within a seamless continuum of conditions. This is not only true of seeds and plants but of the awareness of them as well:

Just as a child is born
From father and mother,
So consciousness springs
From eyes and colorful shapes.

One might intuitively believe "consciousness," the most private and enduring feature of one's self, to be more "real" than the passing phenomena of which it is aware. Consciousness feels like a solitary witness, already there within us, lying in wait for things to appear. For Nagarjuna, this is but a convenient illusion. Consciousness is meaningless unless it is conscious *of* something; it is inextricable from the sense organs and objects that enable it to take place; it is as contingent and ephemeral as the flickering displays of colors and shapes it beholds.

Such reflections lead Nagarjuna to the contingency of human suffering. No matter how real anxiety or depression feel when we are gripped by them, they too can be seen to emerge from a complex set of conditions:

> *Blocked by confusion,*
> *I forge a destiny through impulsive acts.*
> *Consciously I enter situations*
> *Where personality unfolds*
> *And world impacts on a sensitive soul.*

The confusion that "blocks" is that instinctive denial of contingency which simultaneously insists on the presence of a non-contingent self. This creates opposition to an unstable world outside that entices, frightens or bores us. Such responses in turn lead to obsessions with things we crave to have or avoid. The craving crystallizes into clinging to sensual experiences, opinions, rules and selves. Each step further reinforces the pattern of self-obsessively trying to freeze and control reality. "Clinging," says Nagarjuna, "is to insist on being someone."

To understand the contingency of one's experience requires more than just being aware of the present moment as a consequence of the causes and conditions that preceded it. Nagarjuna also speaks of the contingency of oneself and one's attributes. Of the body, he says

I have no body apart
From parts which form it;
I know no parts
Apart from a "body."

Just as we think of an oak tree as different from the acorn that caused it, so do we think of the tree as different from the leaves, branches and trunk that form it now. The body too seems to be one "thing" and its limbs and torso other "things." Yet if we suspend this assumption and observe the body as experienced through the senses, such hard and fast distinctions dissolve. For just as there is no exact time at which one can say the fertilized ovum becomes an embryo, so one can experience no exact point at which the arm becomes a shoulder. We can glimpse the body as an interdependent whole, which is neither the same as nor different from the sum of its parts.

To capture the complex and dynamic nature of cause/effect and part/whole contingency, Nagarjuna meditates on a fire. One imagines him engaged in that timeless act of contemplating a glowing mass of burning fuel on which flames flicker and dance. For Nagarjuna, the fire is a metaphor for human experience: the mass of the fire represents the energetic combustion of mental and physical processes that generate the flickering dance of self. Just as one can distinguish the fire from the flames, so can one distinguish the body-mind from the self. But no clear-cut line can be drawn between them nor can they be regarded as identical:

> *Were the fire its flames,*
> *Act and actor would be one.*
> *Were flames something else,*
> *They could not have lit this fire.*

Nagarjuna questions what it means for flames to be "dependent" on the fire, and vice versa. For even the idea of contingency can suggest a relationship between separate things: one depended on and the other doing the depending. He concludes:

> *Flames do not depend on fires*
> *Nor are they independent of them.*
> *Fires do not depend on flames*
> *Nor are they independent of them.*

Pushed to its limits, the language of contingency itself begins to break down.

Nagarjuna's awareness of contingency includes the role of language in constructing one's sense of reality. He recognizes that experience is "configured" through concepts and words to render it intelligible. To cultivate awareness, one is encouraged to live fully in the present moment, as though the present were somehow more "real" than the past and the future. But the idea of the present is unintelligible without a notion of past and future. In reality there is no such thing as the "present moment." However valuable it may be to try and remain totally in the here and now, one should not mistake a strategy for reducing distraction with a metaphysical statement about the nature of time. As Nagarjuna says

> *Past, present, future*
> *Are like bottom, middle, top*
> *And one, two, three.*

Just as "middle" only makes sense in relation to what is above and below, so "present" only makes sense in relation to what has already gone and what is still to come. The dividing line between them only exists in thought and language; it cannot be found in the sensuous unfolding of life itself. As soon as you let go of fixed ideas of the past and future, the idea of the present evaporates as well. "If life has no beginning and no end, / No before and no after," asks Nagarjuna, "How can it be centered in a present?"

Much of *Verses from the Center* consists of Nagarjuna's

insistent, probing inquiry into life and language. He subjects things and words to a relentless scrutiny, considering them from different angles, in different lights, constantly teasing out their contingency. Toward the end of the work, in the poem *Awakening,* he announces that "contingency is emptiness." To recognize that things are contingent is the key to understanding what it means for them to be empty. A self, a plant, a body or a time is empty because it is incapable of being neatly circumscribed as a thing cut off from other things. Selves, plants, bodies and times are utterly contingent on the complex interplay of conditions, attributes and language with which they are not identical and from which they are not different. To know emptiness is not to negate these things but to be dumbfounded by the sheer fecundity of life.

11

IN THE HOMAGE THAT OPENS *VERSES FROM THE CENTER,* Nagarjuna praises buddhas as those who "teach contingency . . . and ease fixations." The chapters that follow evoke an awareness of contingency not for the sake of establishing a philosophical position, but as a means of easing those fixations that lock one into a life of anguished alienation. In keeping with the Buddha's avowed aim to "show suffering and the ending of suffering," *Verses from the*

Center is a therapeutic critique of those patterns of thought and behavior which provoke and sustain existential unease.

"Fixation" describes the common existential reaction to finding oneself in an unpredictable world. All that is certain in this world is that at some unspecified time one will die. As a means of coping with the anxiety generated by awareness of this fate, human beings elaborate a picture of life in which the self appears to be intrinsically separate from the multitude of other people and things that surround, attract and threaten it. In assuming a safe distance between "me" and "you," and between "me" and "mine," one feels able to manage whatever boring, desirable or terrifying situations face one.

Whatever survival advantages this strategy may have conferred on our early hominid ancestors, it makes us feel cut off from the web of physical and mental processes that sustain life. Depending on the metaphors of our culture, we feel abandoned, cast out of the Garden of Eden, lonely, fragmented, alienated, or trapped in a beginningless cycle of rebirth in which we expend a great deal of energy getting nowhere.

This painful sense of separation is enabled by the capacity of brains and language to construct complex representations of experience. Rather than inhabit the immediate sensory environment, human beings participate in a plurality of worlds (historical, social, economic, religious, psychological, etc.) which extend not only into past and future but across geographic and cultural boundaries. Yet instead of regarding the "self" as a convenient point of reference that allows coherence and continuity among these diverse worlds, the anxious craving for existential security literalizes it into a real, discrete thing.

Fixations about self and things sustain the largely unconscious holding pattern in which we hover above the world of immediate experience. Although fixation appears to freeze the self into an undisturbed, isolated cell, the tightness of its grip spawns chaotic torrents of thoughts, images and emotions. Like squeezing the trigger of a gun or pressing a button to set off an alarm, fixations such as egoism, craving, conceit and opinionatedness erupt as proliferating streams of longings and worries. Even when consciously restrained by a sense of personal and social morality, the insistence and allure of a recurrent fantasy is often sufficient to break whatever resolve one may have had to resist it. One finds oneself thinking, saying and doing things as much out of compulsion as choice.

What may have begun as an uncharacteristically compulsive act can become an addictive form of behavior. The nearer you come to crossing the barrier between a fantasy of seduction and an act of seduction, the more difficult it becomes to desist. The achingly desirable promise of a fantasy is rarely fulfilled in experience. Having achieved our objective, we are left feeling curiously hollow, disappointed, misled. We may not have to wait long, though, before another sequence of images and thoughts begins to stir within this emptiness, luring us toward the next deed.

While affirming the traditional emphasis on the need for self-restraint and love as the basis for moral integrity, Nagarjuna recognizes that a genuine solution to the dilemma of fixation and its concomitant fantasies requires more than adherence to ethical precepts and practices. Although the proliferating thoughts triggered by fixation can be contained by moral commitment and even neutralized by meditative absorption, they are only resolved, according to Nagarjuna, by emptiness:

> *Fixations spawn thoughts*
> *That provoke compulsive acts—*
> *Emptiness stops fixations.*

Although his verses explore and explode assumptions about self, nowhere in *Verses from the Center* does Nagarjuna equate emptiness with the absence or negation of self. This is implicit in the opening verse of his inquiry into self, that prompted Tsongkhapa's enlightenment:

> *Were mind and matter me,*
> *I would come and go like them.*

If I were something else,
They would say nothing about me.

Rather than denying self, Nagarjuna points to its essential ambiguity. He recognizes that for a notion of self to be intelligible, it must provide a sense of constancy amidst change. That is simply what selves are for; it is what they do. Early experiences of one's childhood belong to the person who remembers them many decades later. The passage of life would make no sense if it could not be referred to an unchanging point of reference called "me." We know from photographs and science that nothing remains today of the toddler's body that clutched our favorite toy. And we know from experience that this is even more true of the tearful thoughts and emotions that erupted in our child's mind when the toy was lost.

"If you are what you grasp," says Nagarjuna,

You would not be here.
For what you grasp comes and goes;
It cannot be you.
How can the grasped be the grasper?

Were you identical to the physical and mental traits you think of as yourself, you would be subject to the same changes undergone by the aging body and the fickle mind. But this is not the case. The body may grow wrinkled and fat and have its limbs amputated, while the mind may be overwhelmed by panic attacks or filled with mystical visions, but none of this alters your sense of being the person to whom these things happen.

Nagarjuna is equally aware that the person cannot be understood as *different* from body and mind. For if you were something other than your body and mind, how would your physical or mental traits describe you? Anything that can be thought or said about you is always in relation to a feature of your body or mind. You look in a mirror and comment, "I'm putting on weight." Your partner confirms it. A friend points out that you have a tendency to be late. You reflect on this and recognize that it does indeed describe your behavior. But were you able to remove all your physical and mental characteristics, nothing of "you" would be left. There would no longer be a basis on which to construct even the most tenuous notion of self.

Nagarjuna's verses illuminate this paradoxical nature of self:

> Seeing reveals a seer,
> Who is neither detached
> Nor undetached from seeing.
> How could you see,

And what would you see
In the absence of a seer?

A self or a subject is an integral component of human experience. No matter whether you assume the self to be reducible to some element of experience, insist that it is a disconnected witness of life or deny that it exists at all, in each case you fall prey to the allure of fixation. While such stances might intuitively seem to make sense, they place you in a position which is both logically and existentially untenable.

For Nagarjuna, the Buddha did not preach a doctrine of "no self." What characterizes an awakened perspective is the awareness that any dogmatic position is incompatible with freedom. Nagarjuna remarks:

Buddhas speak of "self"
And also teach "no self"
And also say "there's nothing
Which is either self or not."

Rather than regarding concepts such as "self" and "no self" as the basis of a doctrinal position, which can be upheld or refuted, Nagarjuna treats them as terms within a strategic discourse of freedom, which are employed therapeutically to address the needs of specific situations. Throughout the text, he recognizes that the same is true of any such pair of polarized terms: "same" and "different," "real" and "unreal," "empty" and "not empty," "eternal" and "ephemeral."

To say that "emptiness stops fixations" does not mean that an understanding of something called "emptiness" will suddenly bring to a halt something else called "fixations." Rather than denoting discrete states of mind, the terms "emptiness" and "fixation" suggest *strategies* for living. As strategies they are irreducible to simple definitions. They encompass the complex ways in which we view the world, the values we seek to uphold, the livelihoods in which we are engaged, as well as the social and political structures we hope to develop with others. The crucial difference between strategies of fixation and those of emptiness lies in the fact that the former give rise to anguish, while the latter do not.

Verses from the Center can be understood as Nagarjuna's attempt to illustrate the strategy of emptiness in a range of different contexts. At the heart of his approach lies the recurrent theme of not losing a centered perspective through succumbing to fixated opinions of oneself as either identical or different, eternal or ephemeral, something or nothing:

> *You are not the same as or different from*
> *Conditions on which you depend;*

You are neither severed from
Nor forever fused with them—
This is the deathless teaching
Of buddhas who care for the world.

To have become a person means to have emerged contingently from a matrix of genetic, psychological, social and cultural conditions. You are neither reducible to one or all of them, nor are you separate from them. While a person is *more* than a DNA code, a psychological profile and a social or cultural background, he or she cannot be understood *apart* from such factors. You are unique not because you possess an essential metaphysical quality that differs from the essential metaphysical quality of everyone else, but because you have emerged from a unique and unrepeatable set of conditions.

This "deathless teaching" is traditionally described as one that avoids the extreme positions of eternalism and nihilism. Nagarjuna describes these positions as fixed opinions about oneself:

"I am me, I will never not be"—
The longing for eternity.
"I used to be, I am not any more"—
The cut of annihilation.

As a solution to this dilemma, he points to a middle way in which "the sage avoids being and nothingness." Emptiness does not entail abandoning the dualities of thought and language, but learning to live with them more lightly.

Nagarjuna juggles with the ambiguous and inadequate words he cannot help but use. In one passage he will take it for granted that everything is impermanent, then in another will say that this is a nihilistic view. One moment he will deny that he has an essential nature, only to wonder in the next moment how he could not have one:

If I had an essence,
I would never cease to be me—
My nature could never be anything else.
If I had no essence,
Whose nature would it be to be anything else?

Nagarjuna compares experience to a dream, a stage illusion, a mirage. Such things appear to be real, but on closer inspection turn out to be less real than supposed. Fixations do not manufacture a false reality; they *exaggerate* what is merely contingent. Fixations imbue self and things with a tightness, solidity and opacity. Instead of experiencing the world as an uncertain play of conditions, we prefer the safety of one that appears to be clearcut, predictable and managable. Yet the price to pay for this preference is that life is rendered dull and repetitive. To relieve the tedium, we find ourselves driven to ever more intense moments of experience (food, shopping, drugs, sex, vacations, movies, religion). For Nagarjuna, the problem lies not in the way the world *is* but in the way we have *construed* it.

Loosening this excessive grip on oneself and things does not lead to chaos but to a centered and attentive repose. For while seeming to offer security, fixations generate instability and turmoil. An insistence that self and things are unconnected leads to dissonance and conflict with a world that is deeply interconnected. Since the origins of suffering lie in such misperceptions, the strategy of emptiness entails learning how to see in a way that leads to ease and well-being. Nagarjuna's aim is to change the way one sees in order to transform the quality of one's life. For

> *In seeing things*
> *To be or not to be,*
> *Fools fail to see*
> *A world at ease.*

In a passage in the poem *Self,* Nagarjuna offers a glimpse of the sublime depth disclosed when the constricting hold of fixations is eased:

It is all at ease,
Unfixatable by fixations,
Incommunicable,
Inconceivable,
Indivisible.

Not only is the subjective experience one of ease, but ease is revealed as a feature of the sublime itself. For not only do fixations generate conflict and anguish, they also obscure a natural world that endlessly unfolds and vanishes, untroubled by the desires and fears of humankind. Although we may take our fixations with utmost seriousness, that about which we are fixated is utterly unaffected by them. For life is incapable of ever being tied down. While we generate volumes of theories and descriptions of reality, none can capture the mystery of its happening at all. And no matter how minutely we dissect and categorize experience, the lines we draw leave no trace on the seamless web of life itself.

Nagarjuna's vision is one of uncompromising immanence. What keeps one locked in repetitive cycles of anguish has nothing to do with being cut off from a transcendent God or Absolute or Mind. The classical Buddhist notions of buddhanature and nirvana are treated as metaphors for a freedom that occurs in this very world of sense and reason. Nagarjuna says that

When transfixed
On what's unwavering
Beyond fixation's range,
You see no buddhanature.

Buddhanature
Is the nature of this world.
Buddhanature has no nature,
Nor does this world.

To elevate anything, however noble or exalted, to the status of a transcendent reality beyond this world is fixation's final and yet perhaps most seductive strategy of all.

Fixations are deeply embedded traits of human behavior. They do not magically evaporate the moment one experiences the world as "unfixatable." However liberating such insight may be, it is insufficient to free one from the habit of fixation. Once the intensity of the unfixated moment fades, fixations reassert themselves. Even the experience of freedom itself is not immune to the corruption of fixation. As Nagarjuna is aware:

"I am free! I cling no more!
Liberation is mine!"—
The greatest clinging
Is to cling like this.

A glimpse of freedom does not in itself free one from the craving to be someone special and apart. To be free from such longing entails the patient, ongoing cultivation of an intelligence that is acutely alert to the danger of self-deception. The aim of this process is to go beyond the very need to stand out. As Nagarjuna says,

> *Clinging is to insist on being someone—*
> *Not to cling is to be free to be no one.*

12

EACH CHAPTER OF NAGARJUNA'S *VERSES FROM THE CEN-ter* is an audacious excursion into the sublime landscape of contingency along the track of emptiness. Nagarjuna invites the reader to accompany him along the twists and turns of pathways he has created through this landscape. Just as a path is nothing but a space that has been cleared of those obstacles that prevent freedom of movement across a terrain, so emptiness is nothing but a space cleared of those fixations that prevent freedom of movement through the dilemmas and ambiguities of life. To follow the track of emptiness is to discern the living contours of contingency as they unfold from moment to moment.

The trick is to stumble across one of these pathways in the first place. No matter how much you have thought about emptiness, the living experience of it may have passed you by. Somehow a step has to be made across the gap that separates reason from experience, the head from the heart, metaphysics from poetry. The relentless drive of Nagarjuna's inquiry encourages us to take that step, either by shocking us out of habitual complacency or by slowly wearing down resistance to his vision.

Nagarjuna opens *Verses from the Center* with a reflection on the experience of walking. One imagines him mindfully raising, moving and placing one foot in front of the other as he proceeds slowly along a path. His meditation leads into an ever-deepening perplexity about this unexceptional act:

> *Walking does not start*
> *In steps taken or to come*
> *Or in the act itself.*
> *Where does it begin?*

> *Before I raise a foot,*
> *Is there motion,*
> *A step taken or to come*
> *Whence walking could begin?*

As he contemplates what moves, he realizes that his identity at that moment of being a "walker" is dependent on the movement of his feet. The commonsense assumption that "he" is one thing and his moving feet another is exploded, disclosing an emptiness in which the sheer contingency of his experience is disclosed:

These moving feet reveal a walker
But did not start him on his way.
There was no walker prior to departure.
Who was going where?

Nagarjuna's meditations on the emptiness of common experiences like walking serve as the foundation for his exploration of specific themes of the Buddhist path, such as acts and their effects, buddhanature, the ennobling truths, awakening and nirvana. For Nagarjuna, these ideas are only intelligible through insight into contingency. Yet contingency as an abstract principle does not interest him; it is only significant when revealed as felt, concrete experience:

Without contingency
How could I suffer pain?
This shifting anguish
Has no nature of its own;
If it did, how could it have a cause?

Deny emptiness and you deny
The origins of suffering.

Such existential insight into contingency is tantamount to understanding the four ennobling truths, which Buddhist tradition regards as the components of awakening. "To see contingency," says Nagarjuna, "is to see / Anguish and its origins, / Cessation and the path."

Insight into contingency and emptiness does not add anything to one's store of knowledge about oneself and the world. It reveals an unsuspected dimension of depth which has the capacity to transform one's life. "Emptiness," "contingency," "sublime truth," "buddhanature," "freedom" and "nirvana" denote, for Nagarjuna, different facets of this dimension of depth. Access to this depth is triggered by an urgent, existential process of inquiry that takes place here and now. Rather than a remote transcendent state, nirvana is a liberating relationship to all things. For Nagarjuna, it is simply "the letting go of what rises and passes," and, as such, "is neither something nor nothing." It suggests a freedom that cannot be pinned down in either time or space, prompting Nagarjuna to ask

What do you think
Of a freedom that never happens?

What do you make
Of a life that won't go away?

The intelligence that animates *Verses from the Center* is one that generates and sustains freedom and ease. This experience does not, however, leave one suspended in a vacuum of moral indifference. In his commentary on Nagarjuna's verses, Tsongkhapa quotes a discourse of the Buddha which says, "Whatever depends on conditions is said to be empty. Those who know emptiness are conscientious." This does not mean that emptiness miraculously grants one knowledge of what is the right or wrong thing to do when faced with a moral dilemma. The freedom of emptiness makes one aware of a freedom of choice, for in emptiness one is free—even if only momentarily—from the promptings of fixations that provoke compulsive acts. As the fixated grip of self-centeredness is eased, so also does an empathetic awareness of the suffering of others emerge. The silence of emptiness allows one to hear more clearly the cries of the world.

Nagarjuna argues that only in a contingent and empty world are good and evil possible, for in the frozen world configured by fixations, good or evil deeds would be unable to change anything. Fixations tend to leave one morally numb and indifferent. To gain one's ethical bearings in the dynamic world in which we actually live, it is necessary to ease the fixations that keep us locked in this moral apathy. As a foundation for such an ethics of depth, Nagarjuna recognizes the need to cultivate self-restraint and love and to abide by accepted moral codes as a framework for making decisions.

While Nagarjuna accepts the Buddha's authority on the principles of ethical behavior, he offers his own ideas as to how actions lead to effects in a contingent and uncertain world. Once an act is committed, he argues, it assumes a creative life of its own. "Imagine a magician," he suggests,

Who creates a creature
Who creates other creatures.
Acts I perform are creatures
Who create others.

Once the fateful decision has been made, the words have left our lips or the body's deed is done, the act is released into the flow of life. Its reverberative effects will, to some degree, reconfigure both ourselves and the world in which we encounter the next moral dilemma. The acts we commit now thus form the conditions under which future choices will have to be made.

Although an act is germinated in the privacy of one's thoughts, as soon as it enters the public domain it cannot be retracted or recalled. Nagarjuna declares that

Acts, like contracts,
Are as irrevocable as debts—
Their irrevocability
Ensures fruition.

The consequences of what we do now will outlive us. The irrevocability of our actions implies that we are responsible not only for our own conduct in this life but for the impact of our actions after our death.

The intuitions of the sublime that shimmer through *Versus from the Center* evoke a reality that far outstrips our capacity to represent it adequately in words or concepts. Yet this reality is not, for Nagarjuna, mere chaos. Not only does it unfold in a bewildering variety of organisms that evolve according to natural laws, for human beings it manifests as experiences of pleasure and pain for which we are obliged to assume moral responsibility. For in the very moment we think, speak, or act, we are creating the conditions which will unfold as our personal and collective futures.

Verses from the Center

NAGARJUNA

I bow to buddhas
Who teach contingency
(No death, no birth,
No nothing, no eternity,
No arrival, no departure,
No identity, no difference)
And ease fixations.

Walking

I do not walk between
The step already taken
And the one I'm yet to take,
Which both are motionless.

Is walking not the motion
Between one step and the next?
What moves between them?
Could I not move as I walk?

If I move when I walk,
There would be two motions:
One moving me and one my feet—
Two of us stroll by.

There is no walking without walkers,
And no walkers without walking.
Can I say that walkers walk?
Couldn't I say they don't?

Walking does not start
In steps taken or to come
Or in the act itself.
Where does it begin?

Before I raise a foot,
Is there motion,
A step taken or to come
Whence walking could begin?

What has gone?
What moves?
What is to come?

Can I speak of walkers,
When neither walking,
Steps taken nor to come ever end?

Were walking and walker one,
I would be unable to tell them apart;
Were they different,
There would be walkers who do not walk.

These moving feet reveal a walker
But did not start him on his way.
There was no walker prior to departure.
Who was going where?

Seeing

If my eyes cannot see themselves,
How can they see something else?
Were there no trace of something seen,
How could I see at all?

Neither seeing nor unseeing see.

Seeing reveals a seer,
Who is neither detached
Nor undetached from seeing.
How could you see,
And what would you see
In the absence of a seer?

Just as a child is born
From father and mother,
So consciousness springs
From eyes and colorful shapes.

Without these eyes,
How could I know
Consciousness, impact,
Feeling and thirst?

Clinging, evolving,
Birth, aging and death?

Seers seeing sights explain
Hearers hearing sounds,
Smellers smelling smells,
Tasters tasting tastes,
Touchers touching textures,
Thinkers thinking thoughts.

Body

I have no body apart
From parts which form it;
I know no parts
Apart from a "body."

A body with no parts
Would be unformed,
A part of my body apart from my body
Would be absurd.

Were the body here or not,
It would need no parts.
Partless bodies are pointless.
Do not get stuck in the "body."

I cannot say,
"My body is like its parts."
I cannot say,
"It's something else."

Feelings, perceptions,
Drives, minds, things
Are like this body
In every way.

Conflict with emptiness
Is no conflict;
Objections to emptiness,
No objections.

Space

No trace of space
Is there before
The absence of obstruction
Which describes it.

With no obstruction,
How can there be
Absence of obstruction?
Who distinguishes between them?

Space is not obstruction
Or an absence of it,
Nor is it a description
Or something to describe.

Fluidity and heat,
Energy and gravity
Are just like space.

In seeing things
To be or not to be
Fools fail to see
A world at ease.

Addiction

If an unaddicted addict
Preceded his addiction,
Addiction would depend
On someone unaddicted.

Addicts and addictions go together.

Were addicts and addictions one,
They could not go together;
Were addicts and addictions two,
How would you ever know
They were together?
If they go together,
How can they not be different?

For only different things
Can be together things.
Without differences
Nothing goes together.

Addicts and addictions
Are neither together nor untogether,
Just as all things
Are neither together nor untogether.

Birth

Were birth conditioned
It would be born and live and die
Like all conditioned things.
Were it unconditioned,
How could it describe
Conditioned things?

Does birth give birth
To itself and something else
Like light illuminates
Itself and something else?

Light illuminates
By shedding darkness;
Can light dispel
A dark it never meets?

Were darkness shed
By light it never meets,
A single lamp could lift
The darkness of a galaxy.

If light illuminates
Itself and other things,
Does the dark obscure
Itself and other things?

How can a child
That's not yet born
Give birth to itself?

What has been born,
What's not yet born
And what is being born
Do not give birth.

Everything contingent
Is naturally at ease.

When everyone is dying,
Can I be born and live?
Could I live,
But neither age nor die?

The living are not the dying
Nor the unliving the dying.
Neither milk nor butter
Causes milk to cease.

Something real would never die:
Something can't be nothing.
Nothing too would never die:
You can't behead a person twice.

Actors

Real actors do not perform real acts
Nor unreal actors unreal acts.
Real actors are inactive;
Real acts need no actors.

Real actors do not perform unreal acts
Nor unreal actors real acts.
Unreal acts and unreal actors
Need no causes.

No causes—
No causality.
No causality—
No activity, actors or performance.
No performance—
No good and bad.
No good and bad—
No fruits of good and bad.
No fruits of good and bad—
No way to heaven,
No way to freedom.

Unreal real actors
Do not perform real unreal acts:

Reality and unreality
Cancel each other out.

Actors depend on acts
And acts depend on actors—
I cannot see it otherwise.

When acts and actors vanish,
You understand clinging
And everything else.

Already

Am I already here
Before I see and taste and feel?
If not, how could I see and taste and feel?
How can I know if I'm already here or not?

If I were here without them,
They could be here without me.
I reveal them and they reveal me.
How can I be here without them?
How can they be here without me?

I am not already here
Before experience as such:
Seeing reveals just the seer,
Tasting just the taster,
Feeling just the feeler.

If I'm not already here before them all,
Could I be here before each one?
Can the seer taste?
Can the taster feel?

Were they different,
I would be legion.

Nor am I tucked inside the elements
Whence seeing and tasting and feeling unfold.

If I to whom these things belong
Cannot be found,
How can they be found?
I do not precede them.
Nor am I with them.
Nor do I follow them.

Let go of "I am."
Let go of "I am not."

Fire

Were the fire its flames,
Act and actor would be one.
Were flames something else,
They could not have lit this fire.

Independent and alone,
Eternal flames would burn forever—
Actors with no acts.

Were the fire a fire
Only when it burns—
How could you light this fire?

Were your flames something else,
They would never touch my fire,
Never light it and never die.
They would burn and burn and burn.

Though they are different,
Flames touch fires
As a woman touches a man
And a man a woman.
Flame and fire merge.
They unite despite being different.

If flames depend on fires
And fires upon flames,
What comes first?
Were the fire already there,
The flame that lit it would flare again
Or that fire would flicker flamelessly.

If what flames depend on
Depend on flames,
What depends on what?
How can flames-to-be
Depend on anything?
What would do the depending?

Flames do not depend on fires
Nor are they independent of them.
Fires do not depend on flames
Nor are they independent of them.

Flames and fires explain everything:
The self and what it grasps
And also jugs and rolls of cloth.
Identity and difference? Of self? Of things?

Before

Was there a before before?

If life has no beginning and no end,
No before and no after,
How can it be centered in a present?

Were birth before and death after,
I would be immortal with no history.
Were death first and birth later,
The dead would be unborn.

I cannot be born and die at once:
If birth were death,
They would both be unoriginated.

Why am I transfixed by them?

Anguish

If anguish created itself,
It would not be contingent,
For the pain depends
On what I'm doing now.

Were it other than me
And I other than it,
The pain would be caused
By someone else.

Who am I if I create
My own suffering?
How can I be apart
From pain I cause myself?

Who am I if I can feel
The suffering you create?
Can I be apart
From pain you cause me?

Who are you who hurt me?
How can you be apart
From pain you cause me?

Anguish is not caused by me.
How can it be caused by you?
Anguish caused by you
Is caused by your me too.

Suffering is not caused by me,
For I do not cause myself.
If uncaused by another me,
How could it be caused by you?

If both of us cause pain,
Would not it be caused
By we who have no part in it?
Can anguish be uncaused?

Suffering is nothing special.
Even jugs and rolls of cloth
Do not come from themselves,
Others, both or nothing.

Change

If something has an essence—
How can it ever change
Into anything else?

A thing doesn't change into something else—
Youth does not age,
Age does not age.

If something changed into something else—
Milk would be butter
Or butter would not be milk.

Were there a trace of something,
There would be a trace of emptiness.
Were there no trace of anything,
There would be no trace of emptiness.

Buddhas say emptiness
Is relinquishing opinions.
Believers in emptiness
Are incurable.

Connection

I the beholder,
The one I behold,
The beholding itself
Do not connect with one another—

Just as I who desire,
The one I desire,
The desiring itself
Do not connect.

We do not connect
Because we are not
Apart from one another;
We would not be together

If we were apart.
I am other than you
In relation to you;
I could not be your other without you.

Were I other than you,
Then even without you
I would be someone else;
I cannot be your other without you.

There is no otherness
In either you or me;
Without otherness,
There is no me or you.

I do not connect with me
Nor do I connect with you—
No connecting, no
Connections, no connectors.

Essence

If my essence came
From causes and conditions,
It would have been constructed—
Essences are neither contingent nor contrived.

If I have no essence, how can you?
What is other for me is for you your own—
How can you not be
Yourself or someone else?

Without something,
There could be no nothing—
Do not people say:
A thing becomes nothing
When it changes into something else?

You who behold
Somethings and nothings,
Yourselves and others,
Are blind to what the Buddha taught.

Through understanding
Somethings and nothings,

Gautama told Katyayana
To relinquish being and nothingness.

If I had an essence,
I would never cease to be me—
My nature could never be anything else.
If I had no essence,
Whose nature would it be to be anything else?

"I am me, I will never not be"—
The longing for eternity.
"I used to be, I am not any more"—
The cut of annihilation.

The sage avoids being and nothingness.

Life

Is life what drives me?
Whether constant or fleeting,
Drives are not alive like life.
How am I alive?

When I cannot be found
Inside this mind or body,
Who is there to be alive?
If I survived by clinging on
To thoughts and feelings,
How could I evolve?

Without clinging or evolving,
Who can be alive?
If I came and went,
How could I be freed?

If clinging binds,
I who cling would be unbound
Like those who do not cling.
How is it I am trapped?

Neither bound nor unbound are free—
Were the bound to be freed,

Freedom and bondage
Would be simultaneous.

"I am free! I cling no more!
Liberation is mine!"—
The greatest clinging
Is to cling like this.

What do you think
Of a freedom that never happens?
What do you make
Of a life that won't go away?

Acts

1.

Buddha taught that acts
Are motives of the mind
And words and gestures
You are moved to express.

Restraining yourself
And loving others
Are seeds that bear fruit
In this life and beyond.

2.

If they lasted 'til they ripened,
Acts would be static.
If acts stopped,
How would they bear fruit?

Seeds turn into plants that bear fruit.
Motives turn into minds that bear fruit.
Seeds are neither severed from
Nor forever fused with fruits of plants,
Motives neither severed from
Nor forever fused with fruits of minds.

No killing and no stealing,
No abusing and no lying,
No slandering, swearing, gossiping,
No coveting, resenting or fixating:

These pristine acts
Are ways to practice
That ripen as beauty and pleasure
Here and elsewhere.

3.
Acts, like contracts,
Are as irrevocable as debts—
Their irrevocability
Ensures fruition.

Only patient cultivation
Frees you from their grip—
Insight by itself is insufficient.
Were acts transcended
By understanding—
Insight would destroy them.

Irrevocability alone survives
The vexed transition

From one life to the next—
Emptiness does not negate it;
Life does not set it in stone.

4.

My acts are irrevocable
Because they have no essence.
If they had an essence,
They would be permanent.
No one could have performed them.
I would fear the consequence
Of things I did not do.
I would not lead a noble life.

Descriptions would conflict
With one another.
I would be incapable
Of telling good and bad apart.
Having already ripened,
Acts would ripen again.

If acts are compulsive
And compulsions unreal,
How can acts be real?
Acts and compulsions form me.

What could empty acts
And compulsions form?

Blocked by confusion
Consumers consume the fruits of acts,
Which neither they
Nor anyone else committed.

Where are the doers of deeds
Absent among their conditions?
Where are the fruits of doers and deeds
That cannot be found?
Where are the consumers
Of fruits that are not there?

Imagine a magician
Who creates a creature
Who creates other creatures.
Acts I perform are creatures
Who create others.

Deeds, compulsions, bodies,
Doers, fruits are like
Invisible cities, mirages, dreams.

Self

Were mind and matter me,
I would come and go like them.
If I were something else,
They would say nothing about me.

What is mine
When there is no me?
Were self-centeredness eased,
I would not think of me and mine—
There would be no one there
To think them.

What is inside is me,
What is outside is mine—
When these thoughts end,
Compulsion stops,
Repetition ceases,
Freedom dawns.

Fixations spawn thoughts
That provoke compulsive acts—
Emptiness stops fixations.

Buddhas speak of "self"
And also teach "no self"
And also say "there's nothing
Which is either self or not."

When things dissolve,
There's nothing left to say.
The unborn and unceasing
Are already free.

Buddha said: "it is real,"
And "it is unreal,"
And "it is both real and unreal,"
And "it is neither one nor the other."

It is all at ease,
Unfixatable by fixations,
Incommunicable,
Inconceivable,
Indivisible.

You are not the same as or different from
Conditions on which you depend;
You are neither severed from
Nor forever fused with them—

This is the deathless teaching
Of buddhas who care for the world.

When buddhas don't appear
And their followers are gone,
The wisdom of awakening
Bursts forth by itself.

Time

If I had a past,
What is now and yet to come
Would have already happened.
Were there no now and future then,
How could now and future
Ever have a past?

Without a past
There is no now and future;
What is now and still to come
Would never happen.

Past, present, future
Are like bottom, middle, top
And one, two, three.

You can't grasp time
And times you can
Are never time itself.
Why configure time you cannot grasp?

If time depends on things,
How could I ever have
Time apart from things?
Without things how can time persist?

Disappearance

When you disappear,
You do not appear or fail to appear.
When you appear,
You neither disappear nor fail to disappear.

How can I disappear
Without appearing?
Can I die and not be born?
What disappears appears.

Can I disappear and appear at once?
Do I die the moment I am born?
Can I appear and disappear at once?
Am I born the moment I die?

When everything changes,
How can I appear and not disappear?
Whether dead or alive,
I am neither here nor gone.

Without things,
There would be no appearance or disappearance;
Without which,
There would be no things.

Whether empty or not,
Things neither appear nor disappear.
Appearance and disappearance
Are not the same or different—

They fool you.

Things are not born
From things or nothing,
Nothing is not born
From nothing or things.

If things are either
Eternal or ephemeral,
To believe in them is either
Eternalism or nihilism.

Isn't the appearance
And disappearance
Of seeds and fruits
The flow of life itself?

Seeds would be annihilated:
The disappeared cannot appear again.
You would be erased in nirvana
When the flow of life is stilled.

If life stopped,
How would it start again?
If it never stopped,
How would it start again?

How can it flow
Without flowing before,
Flowing now,
Or flowing later?

Buddhanature

It's not physical, emotional,
Conceptual, impulsive, conscious—
Or anything else.
It does not dwell in us
Nor we in it.
It does not own us.

If it depended on us
Or on anything else,
It would not be in itself.
How could it be anything but itself?
Could what is not itself
Be buddhanature?

What is it apart from itself
Or something else?
Is it independent of body, feeling, thought,
Impulse or consciousness?
It depends on them now
And is set to continue.

Can you say that
Buddhanature is "contingent"

When what is depended on
And what depends are empty?

Can you say that
Buddhanature is "empty"
When "empty" and "not empty"
Are mere ciphers?

Fixed ideas of permanence
And transience,
Finitude and infinity,
Have no place when all is well.

Believers believe in buddhas
Who vanish in nirvana.
Don't imagine empty buddhas
Vanishing or not.

When transfixed
On what's unwavering
Beyond fixation's range,
You see no buddhanature.

Buddhanature
Is the nature of this world.
Buddhanature has no nature,
Nor does this world.

Awakening

The dharma taught by buddhas
Hinges on two truths:
Partial truths of the world
And truths which are sublime.
Without knowing how they differ,
You cannot know the deep;
Without relying on conventions,
You cannot disclose the sublime;
Without intuiting the sublime,
You cannot experience freedom.

Misperceiving emptiness
Injures the unintelligent
Like mishandling a snake
Or miscasting a spell.

The Buddha despaired
Of teaching the dharma,
Knowing it hard
To intuit its depths.

Your muddled conclusions
Do not affect emptiness;
Your denial of emptiness
Does not affect me.

When emptiness is possible,
Everything is possible;
Were emptiness impossible,
Nothing would be possible.

In projecting your faults onto me,
You forget the horse you are riding.

To see things existing by nature,
Is to see them without
Causes or conditions,
Thus subverting causality,
Agents, tools and acts,
Starting, stopping and ripening.

Contingency is emptiness
Which, contingently configured,
Is the middle way.
Everything is contingent;
Everything is empty.

Were everything not empty,
There would be no rising and passing.
Ennobling truths would not exist.
Without contingency
How could I suffer pain?

This shifting anguish
Has no nature of its own;
If it did, how could it have a cause?
Deny emptiness and you deny
The origins of suffering.

If anguish existed by nature,
How would it ever cease?
Absolute misery could never stop.
How could you cultivate a path
That exists by nature?
How could it lead to the end of pain?
A path on which you tread
Can have no essence of its own.

If confusion existed by nature,
I would always be confused.
How could I know anything?
Letting go and realizing,
Cultivation and fruition
Could never happen.

Who can attain absolute goals
That by nature are unattainable?
Since no one could reach them,
There would be no community;

With no truths, no dharma either.
With no community or dharma
How could I awaken?
I would not depend on awakening
Nor awakening on me.

A naturally unawakened person
Would never awaken
No matter how hard
He practiced for its sake.
He would never do good or evil;
An unempty person would do nothing.
He'd experience fruits of good and evil
Without having done good or evil deeds.
How can fruits of good and evil not be empty
If they are experienced?

To subvert emptiness and contingency
Is to subvert conventions of the world.
It engenders passivity:
Acts without an author,
Authors who do not act.
Beings would not be born or die;
They would be frozen in time,
Alien to variety.

If things were unempty,
You could attain nothing.
Anguish would never end.
You would never let go of compulsive acts.

To see contingency is to see
Anguish, its origins, cessation and the path.

Nirvana

Were everything not empty,
Nothing would happen.
Nirvana would be a letting go
And stopping of what?

Nothing let go of, nothing attained,
Nothing annihilated, nothing eternal,
Unceasing and unborn—
That is nirvana.

If it were something,
Nirvana would be contingent
And would wither and die
Like all other things.

Can nirvana be nothing?
Not to be something
Does not mean to be nothing.
Were nirvana nothing,
It would be contingent
Like all other nothings.

Things are created and contingent;
Nirvana is neither:

The letting go of what rises and passes
Is neither something nor nothing.

Were nirvana both something and nothing,
Things and nothings would be free
Or nirvana would be as contingent as they:
Darkness and light cannot be one.

Can I experience nirvana
As neither something nor nothing?
This would be possible
Only if something or nothing were.

After the Buddha died,
He was not seen as existing or not.
Even when he lived
He was not seen as such.

Life is no different from nirvana,
Nirvana no different than life.
Life's horizons are nirvana's:
The two are exactly the same.

Visions of the beyond,
Of eternity, annihilation
Depend on how you see
Nirvana, the past and the future.

What finitude in empty things?
What infinity?
What this? What else?
What stays? What changes?

The dissolving of objects
And easing of fixations is peace.
The Buddha never taught
Anyone anything.

Contingency

Blocked by confusion,
I forge a destiny through impulsive acts.
Consciously I enter situations
Where personality unfolds
And world impacts on a sensitive soul.

Personality creates consciousness
Just as attention,
The eye and a colorful shape
Trigger vision.

Impact is the meeting
Of consciousness, senses and world.
It leads to experience
I crave to have and avoid.
Craving makes me cling
At senses, opinions, rules and selves.

Clinging is to insist on being someone—
Not to cling is to be free to be no one.

To be someone is to be a conscious,
Impulsive, thinking, feeling body,
Which is born, ages, dies,

Suffers torment, grief, pain,
Depression and anxiety.
Anguish emerges when someone is born.

Impulsive acts are the root of life.
Fools are impulsive;
The wise see things as they are.
When confusion stops through insight,
Impulsive acts cease.
Stop this and that will not happen:
Anguish will end.

Opinion

"I was here before."
"No, you weren't."
"This will last forever."—
Horizons of the past.

"I will survive."
"No, you won't."
"This will end."—
Horizons of the future.

What happened in the past
Is not happening any more.
If you think what happened then became you now,
What you grasp would be something else.
What are you but what you grasp?

If you are what you grasp,
You would not be here.
For what you grasp comes and goes;
It cannot be you.
How can the grasped be the grasper?

You're not different from what happened then.
If you were, you would not need a past.

You could survive without having to die.
The past would be severed, revocable.
Others would experience your acts.
Without a past you would be
Either manufactured or uncaused.

"I was here before."
"No, you weren't."
"I was and I wasn't."
"You neither were nor weren't."
"I will survive."
"No, you won't."—

Opinions are absurd.

If the gods were us,
We would be eternal;
For the gods are unborn in eternity.
Were we other than them,
We would be ephemeral.
Were we different,
We would never connect.

If I were half a god and half a man,
I would be eternal and ephemeral.
What can be ephemeral
Without eternity?

If this ends, what world would follow?
If this never ends,
What world would follow?
Like the flame of a lamp
The flow of matter and mind
Neither ends nor never ends.

This would end
If mind and matter failed to flow
From the dying of their past;
It would never end
If mind and matter failed to flow
From a past that never died.

If half this ended and half did not,
I would both end and never end,
Leaving half the grasper
Dead and half undead,
Half the grasped destroyed,
Half undestroyed.

Everything is empty—
In whom? About what?
Do opinions erupt?

For Gautama,
In whose embrace
Dharma was shown
And opinions vanished.

Afterword

Every translation of a classical text is governed by two imperatives: to be faithful to the original, and also to make it intelligible to readers other than those for whom it was written. This tension becomes all the more apparent when working with a text that is not only ancient but from a culture other than one's own. Such a translation cannot but be an interpretation. Just as the Chinese saw Nagarjuna as a kind of Taoist sage, and emptiness as way of speaking about the Tao, so Western translators compare Nagarjuna to figures from their own culture, and emptiness to corresponding ideas in their own preferred philosophical, religious or cultural discourse.

No matter what style, tone or terminology is used, the translator seeks to persuade the reader of his or her authority by giving an impression of a detached, informed and reasonable objectivity. Yet beneath every clear and confident statement on the printed page lie conscious and unconscious layers of unstated beliefs, intuitions, preferences, antipathies, uncertainties and desires.

Work on this book started in the early 1990's with a study of Tsongkhapa's commentary on the chapter *Awakening* (MMK 24) in his *An Ocean of Reason: A Great Exposition of the Root Text* Verses from the Center, written in 1407. This refamiliarized me with both the philosophical tradition of the Tibetan Geluk order (in which I had been trained) and the work of the Indian Centrist commentator Chandrakirti on which it is based.

In 1996 I began a systematic translation of the Tibetan text of *Verses from the Center.* I consulted two editions of the Tibetan (Lhalungpa and Woodblock to Laser) and compared them with the text embedded in the prose of Tsongkhapa's word-by-word commentary. I also read the available English translations from Sanskrit (Streng, Inada and Kalupahana). This enabled me to produce my own edited text of the Tibetan verses, which I translated as literally as possible into English without paying any attention to style. On finishing a chapter, I put the Tibetan aside and treated my literal English translation as the first draft of a poem, which I worked and reworked through numerous drafts until arriving at a text that satisfied me as both consistent with Nagarjuna's original as well as accessible to a contemporary reader.

In an ideal world, I would also have learned Sanskrit, the language in which the original was composed. By choosing to base my translation on another translation, i.e., the Tibetan, I was conscious of losing the philological proximity with Nagarjuna's words that a Sanskrit scholar would have had. At the same time I was aware of working with a text that exists as part of a living Buddhist tradition. From an experiential perspective it was important to me that I could *hear* the text as it would have been spoken by my Tibetan teacher, the late Geshe Rabten. Tibetan tradition understands the nature of a text such as *Verses from the Center* to be that of speech. The printed copy is merely a record of the spoken word; its value is diminished once the oral tradition in that tongue has died out.

Having chosen to emphasize the poetic rather than the philosophical dimension of *Verses from the Center,* my aim throughout was to be able to hear Nagarjuna's voice. I tried to capture the playful and disconcerting quality of his logical moves through wordplay, internal rhymes, jarring contrasts, apparent non sequiturs and unexpected echoes of non-Buddhist sources. I was conscious of influences as diverse as those of John Keats, T. S. Eliot and John Lennon on the formation of my Nagarjunian voice. I was not content with a chapter until I could recite it out loud in a way that (to me at least) caught something of the pulse of emptiness.

A central difficulty for many contemporary readers of Nagarjuna's work is the high degree of abstraction characteristic of Indian Buddhist philosophical writing. I tried to resolve this by making the most of concrete imagery whenever it appeared in the original. Occasionally I introduced a concrete image to flesh out an abstract idea. Although Nagarjuna almost entirely avoids personal pronouns, I tried as much as possible to use the first person "I" as the authorial voice, which enabled me to introduce the second person "you" for the real or hypothetical "other" with whom Nagarjuna is often engaged in dialogue.

The recovery of the poetic threads of the text entailed a rigorous editing of the verses, which resulted in an abridged and adapted translation. Lines, verses and sometimes entire sequences of verses were removed or reordered in this process. At times it seemed that either Nagarjuna or perhaps a later hand had interpolated a passage in order to develop a logical or doctrinal point, which a modern writer would probably have chosen to include as a footnote. Some verses were omitted on the grounds of repetition, others because of obscure doctrinal references, and others simply because I could make little or no sense of them. At other times, though, I expanded the text in order to clarify expressions which Nagarjuna uses as a form of technical shorthand. (The five aggregates [*skandha*], for example, are either listed in full or rendered as "mind and matter.")

Rather than introducing foreign terms or Buddhist neologisms into the fabric of ordinary speech, I sought a contemporary, idiomatic language in which familiar words are surreptitiously invested with new meanings. Likewise, instead of insisting on the same English word throughout to translate a particular term in Tibetan/Sanskrit, I chose to vary the translation as much as possible. *Dukkha,* for example, is translated as "anguish," "suffering," "pain," "misery," etc. This forced me always to consider what word would work best—both in terms of accuracy and style—in any given context. It was also a recognition of the complex range and nuance of Buddhist terms, for which exact equivalents rarely exist in English. Nonetheless, I consistently translated certain key terms which are central to Nagarjuna's vision, such as "emptiness" and "fixation." Tibetan, Sanskrit and Pali equivalents of key terms are given in the glossary that follows.

Central to the Korean Zen Buddhist tradition in which I trained under the late Kusan Sunim is the practice of a *hwadu*. A *hwadu* refers to the central question or dilemma that underpins a koan, i.e., the account of a student's awakening under the guidance or provocation of a Zen master. One of the most famous *hwadu* is "No!" (*mu*)— Chao-chou's response to the question: does a dog have buddhanature? The twelfth-century Korean Zen master Chinul compares the *hwadu* "No!" to "a mass of fire; if you approach it, it burns your face." Nagarjuna's *Verses from the Center* often felt to me like an incandescent shout of "No!" to which my translation was but a stammering response. Nagarjuna constantly reminded me of how my choice of words was contingent both on the fallibility of my understanding and the ambivalence of my motives.

Appendix

Conditions (MMK 1), *Combination* (MMK 20) and *Confusion* (MMK 23).

This translation includes twenty-four chapters out of a total of twenty-seven in the original. The three omitted chapters are *Conditions* (MMK 1), *Combination* (MMK 20) and *Confusion* (MMK 23), which are translated here. The reason for the omission of these chapters from the main body of the translation is primarily a literary one. I found that their removal restored an organic unity to the unfolding of Nagarjuna's vision. I felt that these chapters hindered the poetic flow and coherence of the text. In contrast to the other chapters, they also proved more resistant to being rendered in a contemporary and idiomatic style.

Conditions, traditionally the opening chapter, is uncharacteristically doctrinaire. It could be a later addition, designed to impress the reader with an unequivocal statement of Nagarjuna's "position." Its tone and subject matter are in striking contrast to the immediacy of the chapters that follow: *Walking, Seeing, Body,* etc. *Combination* and *Confusion* are illuminating but lengthy digressions from the trajectory and pace of Nagarjuna's core inquiry. In terms of content, all three chapters are consistent with the rest of *Verses from the Center.*

Conditions

Nothing comes from itself
Or something else
Or both together
Or without a cause.

The essence of a thing
Is never to be found
In causes or precursors,
Consciousness or objects—
For if a thing is not itself,
How can it be something else?

I too did not appear
Either with conditions
Or without them:
They became my conditions
Only when I sprang from them,
Not before.

Whether I am there or not,
Conditions are impossible—
For in my absence,
Whose conditions would they be?

And in my presence,
What purpose would they serve?

You cannot say:
"When this is present, that happens"—
For the presence of an inessential thing
Is never to be found.

How can conditions cause
Something unconnected to them?
Why could I not have been born
From causes that were not my conditions?

How could my nature be conditioned
When conditions have no nature of their own?
How could it ever be my nature
To be without conditions?

Combination

If fruits are in the seed,
Why would they have to grow
From a combination
Of seed and earth,
Water, heat and air?
Were they not in their causes,
How could they originate
From a cluster of causes?

If fruits are in the seed,
You should be able to find them there.
If they are not there,
How does mango seed
Differ from plantain seed?

If seed stopped the moment it bore fruit,
It would be schizoid seed:
Halting and starting.
If it stopped before fruition,
Its mangos would be unoriginated.

If mangos appear
When causes combine,
Creator and created would be one.

If mangos precede the combining,
They would need no cause.

If, when causes stop,
They are transferred to their fruits,
Seeds created before
Would be created again.

How can mangos appear
From the vanishing of their seed?
How can they appear
While their seed is present?
How can they appear
Unconnected to seed?

Seeds neither witness nor do not witness
Mangos they create:
Without connecting with mangos,
How can seed create them?
Through connecting with mangos,
How can it create them?

How can seed, empty of mangos,
Create mangos?
How can seed, not empty of mangos,
Create mangos?

How can seed create empty mangos?
How would they stop?
Empty and unempty mangos
Are uncreatable and unstoppable.

If mangos were real,
What could their seed create?
If mangos were unreal,
What could their seed create?

An uncreating cause
Is not a cause.
With no cause,
Whose fruit would mangos be?

If a cluster of causes
Cannot create itself,
How can it create mangos?
Mangos are not created
By their combination
Or their uncombination.
What combination of conditions?
There are no mangos.

Confusion

Concepts are at the root of it:
Greed, hatred, bewilderment
Depend on what is conceived
As desirable, despicable or confusing.

How can such things trouble me
If they are not what they seem?
Without anyone to trouble,
Compulsions would be no one's.

The concept "body"
Is not inside my flesh and bones,
Just as these compulsions
Are not inside my troubled soul.
Nor are my flesh and bones
Inside the concept "body";
Nor is my troubled soul
Inside its compulsions.

If what is "desirable,"
"Despicable" and "confusing"
Have no nature of their own,
Why do they trouble me?
I may believe that objects of the senses

Are the foundations of desire—
But they are like invisible cities,
Mirages and dreams.

Are they desirable or despicable?
"Desirable" and "despicable"
Depend on each other;
Neither stands alone.
If nothing is desirable,
How can I covet it?
If nothing is despicable,
How can I hate it?

Manners of conception,
Conceptuality itself,
Conceived and conceiver
Are all at ease.
When there is no confusion
And no unconfusion,
Who is confused and who is not?
Work that out for yourself.

If self, incorruptibility,
Eternity and happiness were real,
They would not confuse me.
Were they unreal,

Nor would selflessness,
Corruption, transience or anguish.
In ending confusion, ignorance stops
And compulsive acts cease.

If there were a problem,
How could I be rid of it?
Who can destroy what is real?
If there were no problem,
How could I be rid of it?
Who can destroy the unreal?

Notes

NB. *"MMK" refers to the* Mūlamadhyamakakārikā. *The numbers that follow refer to chapter and verse number as found in standard editions and translations of the text. Thus "MMK 18:24" refers to chapter 18, verse 24. For more literal translations of the verses, see Kalupahana's* Nāgārjuna: The Philosophy of the Middle Way *and Garfield's* The Fundamental Wisdom of the Middle Way.

Intuitions of the Sublime

1.

p. 3 . . . **Behind the gilded Swayambu stupa** . . . This opening section is based on field research done in October 1994. I am indebted to Keith Dowman for his help in locating these sites.

p. 6 ... **If the gods were us,** ... See *Opinion* (MMK 27:15–16).

p. 6 ... **What is ephemeral** ... See *Opinion* (MMK 27:17).

2.

p. 7 ... **It was not until Greek settlers in India converted to Buddhism** ... See Batchelor, *The Awakening of the West,* 14–15.

p. 8 ... **"What is liberation of mind through emptiness?"** See the *Mahāvedalla Sutta,* in the *Middle Length Discourses of the Buddha* (M. 43:33), 394 (adapted).

p. 9 ... **the "abode of a great person** ..." See the *Piṇḍāpatapārisuddhi Sutta,* in the *Middle Length Discourses of the Buddha* (M. 151:2), 1143.

p. 9 ... **"How is it, Venerable Gautama; does the self exist?"** Quoted in Ñāṇamoli Thera. *The Life of the Buddha,* 209–10 (adapted). The source is *Saṁyutta Nikāya* 12: 17.

p. 11 ... **Katyayana, everyday experience relies** ... From the *Questions of Kātyāyana,* as translated by Huntingdon, *The Emptiness of Emptiness,* 37. This short discourse is also found in the Saṁyutta Nikāya of the Pali Canon as the *Kaccāyanagotta-sutta* (S. 2:17). For a complete translation from the Pali, see Kalupahana, *Nāgārjuna: The Philosophy of the Middle Way,* 10–11.

3.

p. 12 ... **an empty vessel** ... See Waley, *The Way and its Power,* 146.

p. 12 . . . **a bellows / In that it is empty** . . . See Waley, *The Way and its Power,* 147.

p. 12 . . . **subtracting day by day** . . . See Waley, *The Way and its Power,* 201.

p. 12 . . . **What is the fasting of the mind?** See Watson, *Chuang Tzu: Basic Writings,* 54.

p. 13 . . . **I came at him empty,** . . . See Watson, *Chuang Tzu: Basic Writings,* 94.

p. 14 . . . **This doctrine remained a source of controversy between Buddhists and Taoists** . . . See Ch'en, *Buddhism in China,* 50–3.

4.

p. 14 . . . **the first known account of Nagarjuna's life was composed from Indian sources by Kumarajiva** . . . See Walleser, *The Life of Nāgārjuna from Tibetan and Chinese Sources* and Robinson, *Early Mādhyamaka in India and China.* Kumarajiva, an almost exact contemporary of St. Augustine, was born in 344 C.E. in Kucha, a thriving commercial and cultural city in Central Asia, to an Indian father and a Kuchean princess. When he was nine years old, his mother, who had become a nun, took him to India to study in the monasteries of the early Buddhist schools. Three years later they returned to Central Asia, where Kumarajiva was converted to Mahayana Buddhism and became a prominent scholar-monk in Kucha. He was captured by a Chinese warlord and taken to China, and spent the last twelve years of his life in the capital,

Chang-an (Xian), where he translated a total of seventy-two Buddhist texts, including *Verses from the Center* and several *Wisdom Discourses*. He died in 413.

p. 17 . . . **The *Wisdom Discourses* . . . are a series of inspirational dialogues** . . . Although Mahayana tradition regards Nagarjuna's *Verses from the Center* as a commentary to the *Wisdom Discourses*, since the verses do not refer to them, it makes as much sense to consider the *Wisdom Discourses* as extended commentaries to *Verses from the Center*. The legend of Nagarjuna retrieving these texts from the *naga*s would have realized two aims: it explained why such discourses were previously unknown in India, and at the same time enabled the Mahayanists to co-opt the influential Nagarjuna into their camp.

p. 18 . . . ***Questions of Katyayana*** . . . Nagarjuna cites it in *Essence* (MMK 15:7). See notes to section 2 above for details on this discourse. The ***Questions of Kashyapa*** (*KāshyapaparivartaSūtra*) is part of the Ratnakūta collection of Mahayana Discourses. See Warder, *Indian Buddhism*, 357. Nagarjuna refers to it in the final verse of *Change* (MMK 13:8)—see the note to *Change* below.

p. 19 . . . **Since the Buddha compared this sage to a naga,** . . . see the *Vammika Sutta* in *Middle Length Discourses of the Buddha* (M. 23), 239: "The Nāga serpent is a symbol for a bhikkhu who has destroyed the taints. 'Leave the Nāga serpent; do not harm the Nāga serpent; honour the Nāga serpent.' This is the meaning." This point is made by Stcherbatsky in *The Conception of Buddhist Nirvana*, 5.

p. 19 . . . **When buddhas don't appear** . . . See *Self* (MMK 18:12).

p. 20 . . . **Whoever else he may have been** . . . Although *Verses from the Center* sheds no light on Nagarjuna's subsequent fate with the king, another text attributed to him is addressed to a king called Gautamiputra, one of the founders of the Satvahana dynasty. This text, known as the *Friendly Letter,* consists of an account of Buddhist practice from the perspective of early tradition in the form of advice to a layman from a monk. As with *Verses from the Center,* there is no mention of either the Mahayana, the bodhisattva or the *Wisdom Discourses.* While the terms "Mahayana" and "bodhisattva" are not used, the text does contain a reference to the Mahayana doctrine of the six perfections and, toward the end, mentions Avalokiteshvara (the bodhisattva of compassion) and the Pure Land Paradise of the Buddha Amitabha, which suggests familiarity with early Mahayana devotionalism. See Nagarjuna. Tr. Lozang Jamspal et al., *Nāgārjuna's Letter to King Gautamīputra.* Another letter to a king, called the *Precious Garland (Ratnāvalī),* is also attributed to Nagarjuna, but the polemical style of this sectarian Mahayana work is entirely at odds with *Verses from the Center.*

p. 21 . . . **Contingency is emptiness** . . . See *Awakening* (MMK 24:18).

p. 21 . . . **When emptiness is possible,** . . . See *Awakening* (MMK 24:14). Cf. also *Vigrahavyāvartanī* LXX.

p. 21 . . . **Were there a trace of something,** . . . See *Change* (MMK 13:7).

p. 22 . . . **Buddhas say emptiness / Is relinquishing opinions.** See *Change* (MMK 13:8).

p. 22 . . . **Nagarjuna compares emptiness to a poisonous snake** . . . See *Awakening* (MMK 24:11). The Buddha uses this metaphor in relation to the dharma itself. See *The Simile of the Snake* (*Alagaddūpama Sutta*) in the *Middle Length Discourses of the Buddha* (M. 22:10–12), 227–8.

p. 23 . . . **Believers believe in buddhas** . . . See *Buddhanature* (MMK 22:13–14).

5.

p. 24 . . . **These three texts formed the basis** . . . In addition to *Verses from the Center*, Kumarajiva translated or more probably compiled the *Twelve Topics*, a prose summary of *Verses from the Center,* and the *Great Wisdom Treatise*, a voluminous encyclopedia of doctrines, legends and citations, including more than forty of Nagarjuna's verses scattered through the text.

p. 25 . . . **Emperor Wu of Liang asked the great master Bodhidharma,** . . . This is the first koan in *The Blue Cliff Record*. See Cleary and Cleary, *The Blue Cliff Record,* 1 (adapted).

p. 26 . . . **Your disciple's mind is not yet at peace!** This is case forty-one in the *Gateless Gate*. See Yamada, *Gateless Gate*, 208.

p. 27 . . . **Do not sit with a mind fixed on emptiness.** See Yampolsky, *The Platform Sutra of the Sixth Patriarch*, 146.

p. 28 . . . **SHIH-KUNG: Can you grasp emptiness?** See Kim, *Dogen Kigen—Mystical Realist*, 172 (adapted).

p. 29 . . . **play in emptiness.** See Kim, *Dogen Kigen—Mystical Realist*, 114.

p. 29 . . . **like a hammer striking emptiness** . . . See Tanahashi, *Moon in a Dewdrop*, 147.

p. 29 . . . **You must surely know emptiness is a perfect grass.** See Kim, *Dogen Kigen—Mystical Realist*, 117.

p. 30 . . . **To study the Way . . . is to study oneself** . . . See Kim, *Dogen Kigen—Mystical Realist*, 133, and Yasutani, *Flowers Fall*, 102–3 (adapted).

6.

p. 31 . . . **a lightning flash on a dark cloudy night** . . . See Shāntideva, *A Guide to the Bodhisattva's Way of Life / The Bodhicaryāvatāra*, 1:5.

p. 31 . . . **a blind man who has found a jewel** . . . Ibid. 3:28.

p. 31 . . . **Was it not crazy** . . . Ibid. 4:42.

p. 31 . . . **wide open places devoid of any sense of "mine"** . . . Ibid. 8:27.

p. 32 . . . **Just as these arms and legs** . . . Ibid. 8:114.

p. 34 . . . **I should dispel the pain of others** . . . Ibid. 8:94–6 (abridged).

p. 34 . . . **When I act for the sake of others,** . . . Ibid. 8:116.

p. 35 . . . **When neither something nor nothing** . . . Ibid. 9:34.

7.

p. 37 . . . **Five hundred years later, in the late spring of 1398,** . . . Cf. Robert Thurman. *Tsong Khapa's Speech of Gold in the* Essence of True Eloquence, 84–5.

p. 37 . . . **Were mind and matter me,** . . . See *Self* (MMK 18:1).

p. 38 . . . **the body that serves as the foundation for all Centrist treatises** . . . See Tsongkhapa, *An Ocean of Reason*, 16.

p. 39 . . . **Tsongkhapa and his followers sought to define "emptiness"** . . . The definitive account in English of the Geluk understanding of emptiness is Jeffrey Hopkins' *Meditation on Emptiness*.

p. 40 . . . **the Geluk monk Shabkar Tsoknyi Rangdrol,** . . . For further information on this remarkable monk, see Matthieu Ricard (tr.), *The Life of Shabkar*.

p. 41 . . . **Now come up close and listen.** See Shabkar, *'Od gsal rdzogs pa chen po'i khregs chod lta ba'i glu dbyangs sa lam ma lus myur du bgrod pa'i rtsal ldan mkha' lding gshog rlabs*, fol. 7b–8a. Also Dowman, *The Flight of the Garuda*, 87–8.

p. 42 . . . **Having stripped awareness naked** . . . Ibid. 28a–b. Also Dowman, ibid., 125.

p. 42 . . . **When all I do is think about reality** . . . See Shabkar, *'Od gsal rdzogs pa chen po'i lhun grub thod rgal gyi glu dbyangs ting 'dzin sgo 'phar brgya phrag gcig car 'byed pa'i lde'u mig*, fol. 37b–38b.

p. 43 . . . **the solitude of a mountain peak** . . . Ibid. fol. 43a–b.

8.

p. 44 . . . **the least of an egoist that it was possible to be** . . . Quoted in Motion, *Keats*, 227. Keats was commenting on a January 1818 lecture by William Hazlitt that he had recently heard: "Hazlitt's favourite doctrine, and the subject of his first book, was 'the natural disinterestedness of the human mind.' . . . 'It cannot be concealed,' Hazlitt said, 'that the progress of knowledge and refinement has a tendency to circumscribe the limits of the imagination, and to clip the wings of poetry.' Keats developed this into a faith in the 'self-annulling character' of the poet. . . . it informs his notion of negative capability . . ." Motion, 125.

p. 44 . . . **As to the poetical Character itself** . . . From a letter of 27 October 1818. See Gittings, *Selected Poems and Letters of John Keats*, 87. This idea resurfaces, for example, in Maurice Blanchot: "The writer belongs to a language which no one speaks, which is addressed to no one, which has no center, and which reveals nothing. He may believe that he affirms himself in this language, but what he affirms is altogether deprived of self." (*The Space of Literature,* 26.) A similar sentiment is found in Mark Rothko's comment, "I don't express myself in my painting, I express my not-self." (Quoted in Breslin, *Mark Rothko: A Biography*, 273–4. Thanks to David Batchelor for this reference.)

p. 45 . . . **Negative Capability** . . . From a letter of 21 December 1817. See Gittings, *Selected Poems and Letters of John Keats*, 40–1.

p. 45 . . . **a Ch'an/Zen practice in which the meditator settles into a state of perplexity** . . . See Batchelor, *The Faith to Doubt*, 19–58.

p. 46 . . . **suspension of the Act of Comparison** . . . Quoted in Holmes, *Coleridge: Darker Reflections*, 130. Coleridge later developed this idea into his famous expression "the willing suspension of disbelief."

p. 46 . . . **by alternate pulses of active and passive motion** . . . Quoted in Holmes, *Coleridge: Darker Reflections*, 397.

p. 46 . . . **Neither Keats nor Coleridge knew anything about Buddhism** . . . The first Sanskrit Buddhist texts did not arrive in Europe until 1837, three years after Coleridge's death. These consisted mainly of the Buddha's *Wisdom Discourses* and also included *Clear Words*, Chandrakirti's verse-by-verse analysis of Nagarjuna's *Verses from the Center*. In the same year, the *Diamond Cutter*, which had awakened Huineng as a boy, became the first Buddhist discourse to appear in a European language, translated into French from Tibetan by the Russian Isaak Jakob Schmidt.

p. 47 . . . **at other times I adopt the Brahman Creed,** . . . Quoted in Drew, *India and the Romantic Imagination,* 188. ("Vishna" and "Lotos" are Coleridge's spellings.) Until the end of his life Coleridge was greatly influenced by the work of the translator, editor and literary theorist, August Wilhelm von Schlegel. Schlegel not only translated seventeen of Shakespeare's plays, he founded Sanskrit studies in Germany and edited the *Ramayana* and the *Bhagavadgita*.

p. 47 . . . **thunders and howling of the breaking ice,** . . . Quoted in Holmes, *Coleridge: Early Visions*, 230. Although the notion of the sublime was analyzed in the West by a contemporary of Nagarjuna called Longinus, it was not until the eighteenth century that it was recovered from obscurity. Two books were primarily responsible for this: Edmund Burke's *Philosophical Inquiry into the Origin of our Ideas of the Sublime and Beautiful* (1757) and Immanuel Kant's *Critique of Aesthetic Judgement* (1790). Burke in particular was keenly discussed in the circles of the English Romantic poets. In relation to Nagarjuna and his legend, it is noteworthy that Burke regarded both serpents and the ocean as sources of the idea of the sublime.

p. 49 . . . **like a lion pierced deeply in the heart** . . . Ashvaghosa. *Buddhacarita* V:1. For a more detailed reading of this legend of the Buddha, see my *Alone With Others: An Existential Approach to Buddhism*, 30—9.

p. 49 . . . **The Buddha despaired** . . . See *Awakening* (MMK 24:12).

p. 49 . . . **Without knowing how they differ** . . . See *Awakening* (MMK 24:10—11).

p. 51 . . . **Life is no different from nirvana,** . . . See *Nirvana* (MMK 25:19—20). These words of Nagarjuna find a curious echo in an essay written by the American painter Barnett Newman in 1948 entitled "The Sublime is Now." By renouncing all forms of representation in favor of pure abstraction, Newman seeks to embody rather than depict the sublime. The emptiness of his paintings both shocks and absorbs the viewer. "The inexpressible," comments the French philosopher Jean-François Lyotard in a discussion of Newman's work, "does not reside in an over there, in another world, or another time, but in this: in that something happens." Quoted in Berry and Wernick, *Shadow of Spirit*, 15.

10.

p. 55 . . . **Seeds turn into plants that bear fruit.** See *Acts* (MMK 17:7–10).

p. 56 . . . **Just as a child is born** . . . See *Seeing* (MMK 3:7).

p. 57 . . . **Blocked by confusion,** . . . See *Contingency* (MMK 26:1–3).

p. 57 . . . **Clinging . . . is to insist on being someone.** See *Contingency* (MMK 26:7).

p. 58 . . . **I have no body apart** . . . See *Body* (MMK 4:1).

p. 59 . . . **Were the fire its flames,** . . . See *Fire* (MMK 10:1).

p. 59 . . . **Flames do not depend on fires** . . . See *Fire* (MMK 10:12).

p. 60 . . . **Past, present, future** . . . See *Time* (MMK 19:4).

p. 60 . . . **If life has no beginning and no end,** . . .
See *Before* (MMK 11:2).

p. 61 . . . **contingency is emptiness.** See *Awakening*
(MMK 24:18).

11.

p. 61 . . . **Nagarjuna praises buddhas as those who
". . . ease fixations."** Fixation (*prapañca*) is a key term in
Verses from the Center. For an analysis of its meaning in the early
Buddhist canon, see Ñānananda, *Concept and Reality, passim*, and
Hamilton, *Identity and Experience,* 55–7. Tsongkhapa glosses it
as "conceptually grasping [something] as truly existent" (*bden
par zhen pa'i spros pa*). See *An Ocean of Reason,* 322.

p. 64 . . . **Fixations spawn thoughts** . . . See *Self*
(MMK 18:5).

p. 64 . . . **Were mind and matter me,** . . . See *Self*
(MMK 18:1).

p. 65 . . . **If you are what you grasp** . . . See *Opinion*
(MMK 27:4–5).

p. 66 . . . **Seeing reveals a seer,** . . . See *Seeing* (MMK 3:6).

p. 67 . . . **Buddhas speak of "self"** . . . See *Self* (MMK 18:6).

p. 68 . . . **You are not the same as or different
from** . . . See *Self* (MMK 18:11).

p. 69 . . . **"I am me, I will never not be"** . . . See
Essence (MMK 15:11).

p. 70 . . . **Emptiness does not entail abandoning the
dualities of thought and language, but learning to**

live with them more lightly. Both the Buddha in the *Dhammapada* and Shāntideva in the *Bodhicaryāvatāra* compare the practitioner to a bee who delicately extracts the nectar from a flower, then departs without leaving a trace.

p. 70 . . . **In one passage [Nagarjuna] will take it for granted that everything is impermanent, then in another will say that this is a nihilistic view.** See *Disappearance* (MMK 21:14).

p. 70 . . . **If I had an essence,** . . . See *Essence* (MMK 15:8-9).

p. 71 . . . **In seeing things** . . . See *Space* (MMK 5:8).

p. 72 . . . **It is all at ease,** . . . See *Self* (MMK 18:9).

p. 73 . . . **When transfixed** . . . See *Buddhanature* (MMK 22:15–16).

p. 73 . . . **"I am free! I cling no more!"** See *Life* (MMK 16:9).

p. 74 . . . **Clinging is to insist on being someone** . . . See *Contingency* (MMK 26:7).

12.

p. 74 . . . **the track of emptiness** . . . Tsongkhapa described emptiness as "the track on which the centered person moves." See Tsongkhapa, *An Ocean of Reason*, 431. This is part of his commentary to MMK 24:18. See also Batchelor, *Buddhism Without Beliefs*, 80–1.

p. 75 . . . **Walking does not start** . . . See *Walking* (MMK 2:12–13).

p. 76 . . . **These moving feet reveal a walker** . . . See *Walking* (MMK 2:22).

p. 76 . . . **Without contingency** . . . See *Awakening* (MMK 24:21–22).

p. 77 . . . **To see contingency** . . . **is to see** . . . See *Awakening* (MMK 24:40). These lines are reminiscent of the Buddha's axiomatic statement, "One who sees contingency sees the dharma; whoever sees the dharma sees the buddha." Quoted in Tsongkhapa, *An Ocean of Reason*, 174. Cf. The *Mahā-hatthipadopama Sutta*, in *The Middle Length Discourses of the Buddha*, 283 (M. 28:28).

p. 77 . . . **the letting go of what rises and passes** . . . See *Nirvana* (MMK 25:10).

p. 77 . . . **What do you think** . . . See *Life* (MMK 16:10).

p. 78 . . . **Whatever depends on conditions is said to be empty.** See Tsongkhapa, *An Ocean of Reason*, 175. The discourse from which it is cited is the *Questions of Madrosava* [sp. ?], which almost certainly belongs to the Mahayana canon.

p. 79 . . . **Nagarjuna recognizes the need to cultivate self-restraint and love** . . . See sections 1 and 2 of *Acts* (MMK 17).

p. 79 . . . **Imagine a magician** . . . See *Acts* (MMK 17:31–2).

p. 80 . . . **Acts, like contracts,** . . . See *Acts* (MMK 17:14–15).

Verses from the Center

Conditions are unreal
Because they deceive you—
Therefore they are empty.

Things have no essence
Because they change into other things—
Emptiness is their essence.

Without an essence—
Whose nature would it be
To change into anything else?

This recalls a passage from the *Dhātuvibhanga Sutta* in the *Middle Length Discourses of the Buddha* (M. 140), 1093: "For that is false, *bhikkhu*, which has a deceptive nature, and that is true which has an undeceptive nature—*Nibbana*." Since the second part of the chapter is a rebuttal of this view and concludes with a reference to the *Kāshyapaparivarta Sūtra,* an early Mahayana text, this would be a clear instance of Nagarjuna's sympathy for the newly emerging movement. I am indebted to some unpublished translations by Jeffrey Hopkins of selected verses for this reference.

p. 104 **Connection.** A translation of MMK 14—Analysis of Connections.

p. 106 **Essence.** A translation of MMK 15—Analysis of Essence.

p. 108 **Life.** A translation of MMK 16—Analysis of Bondage and Freedom.

The original text opens with an objection, which Nagarjuna then refutes point by point. I have not included this, nor the opening stanza of Nagarjuna's rebuttal. The passage is an uncharacteristically formal and didactic device. It reads as follows:

"If everything is empty,
There would be no rising and passing.
Ennobling truths would not exist.
There would be no understanding,
Letting go, cultivating, realizing.
Without tasting the fruits of practice,
There would be no community;
With no truths, no dharma either.
With no community and dharma,
How could you awaken?
Talk of emptiness maligns what is of value.

Acts and fruits, good and evil,
Conventions fall apart."

Not knowing emptiness,
The need for it
Or the point of it,
You subvert it.

This entire chapter might have initially been an autonomous essay. It seems aimed at a specific public in a way that none of the other chapters does, and has an oddly pointed rhetorical tone. Of the thirty-seven instances of the word "emptiness" in *Verses from the Center*, fifteen are found in this chapter.

p. 128 **Nirvana.** A translation of MMK 25—Analysis of Nirvana. Like *Awakening*, this chapter opens with a hypothetical objection, which is merely the opposite of Nagarjuna's view. It reads:

Were everything empty,
Nothing would happen.
Nirvana would be a letting go
And stopping of what?

p. 131 **Contingency.** A translation of MMK 26—Analysis of the Twelve Links of Dependent Origination. Although I have retained this poem in the main body of the text, its style and explicit doctrinal content suggest that it could have been a later addition.

p. 133 **Opinion.** A translation of MMK 27—Analysis of Views.

p. 136 . . . **For Gautama, In whose embrace** . . . Tsongkhapa observes that although this homage is included as the final verse in *Opinion* (MMK 27), it can be treated separately in recognition of the fact that everything taught in *Verses from the Center* is contingent on the kindness of the Buddha. See *An Ocean of Reason*, 480.

Colophon

p. 142 . . . **a mass of fire; if you approach it, it burns your face.** See Buswell, *The Korean Approach to Zen*, 239.

Appendix

p. 145 **Conditions.** A translation of MMK 1—Analysis of Conditions.

p. 147 **Combination.** A translation of MMK 20—Analysis of Combination.

p. 150 **Confusion.** A translation of MMK 23—Analysis of Error.

Glossary

English	Tibetan	Sanskrit	Pali
act	*las*	*karma*	*kamma*
awakening	*byang chub*	*bodhi*	*bodhi*
compulsion	*nyon mongs*	*kleśa*	*kilesa*
configure	*btags ba*	*prajñapti*	—
contingency	*rten cing 'brel ba 'byung ba*	*pratītyasam- utpāda*	*paṭiccasam- uppāda*
ease	*zhi ba*	*śānti*	*santi*
emptiness	*stong pa nyid*	*śūnyatā*	*suññata*
fixation	*spros pa*	*prapañca*	*papañca*
freedom	*mya ngan las 'das pa*	*nirvāna*	*nibbāna*

intelligence	*shes rab*	*prajñā*	*paññā*
liberated sage	*'gra bcom pa*	*arhat*	*arahat*
life	*'khor ba*	*saṃsāra*	*saṃsāra*
partial truth	*kun rdzob bden pa*	*saṃvṛtisatya*	*sammutisacca*
self	*bdag*	*ātman*	*attā*
sublime truth	*don dam bden pa*	*paramārtha-satya*	*paramattha-sacca*
wisdom	*shes rab gyi pha rol tu phyin pa*	*prajñāpāram-itā*	—

Bibliography

Batchelor, Stephen. *Alone With Others: An Existential Approach to Buddhism.* New York: Grove, 1983.

—. *The Awakening of the West: The Encounter of Buddhism and Western Culture.* Berkeley: Parallax, 1994.

—. *Buddhism Without Beliefs: A Contemporary Guide to Awakening.* New York: Riverhead, 1996.

—. *The Faith to Doubt: Glimpses of Buddhist Uncertainty.* Berkeley: Parallax, 1990.

Bhattacharya, Kamaleswar. *The Dialectical Method of Nāgārjuna* (Vigrahavyāvartanī). Delhi: Motilal Banarsidass, 1978.

Blanchot, Maurice. Tr. Ann Smock. *The Space of Literature.* Lincoln: University of Nebraska Press, 1982 (first published 1955).

Berry, Philippa, and Wernick, Andrew (eds.). *Shadow of Spirit: Postmodernism and Religion*. London: Routledge, 1992.

Breslin, James E. B. *Mark Rothko: A Biography*. Chicago: Chicago University Press, 1993.

Buddha. Tr. Narada Maha Thera. *The Dhammapada*. Calcutta: Maha Bodhi Society of India, 1970.

—. Tr. Bhikkhu Ñāṇamoli and Bhikkhu Bodhi. *The Middle Length Discourses of the Buddha: A New Translation of the Majjhima Nikāya*. Boston: Wisdom, 1995.

Burke, Edmund. Ed. David Wormersley. *A Philosophical Enquiry into the Sublime and the Beautiful*. London: Penguin, 1998.

Buswell, Robert. *The Korean Approach to Zen: The Collected Works of Chinul*. Honolulu: University of Hawaii Press, 1983.

Chandrakirti. *Guide to the Center (Madhyamakāvatāra)*. Tibetan: *dBu ma la 'jug pa*. Varanasi: Legs bshad gter mdzod par khang, 1972. Translated by C. W. Huntington in *The Emptiness of Emptiness* (see below). A partial translation is found in Geshe Rabten, *Echoes of Voidness* (see below).

—. *Clear Words (Prasannapadā)*. Tibetan: *dBu ma rtsa she'i 'grel pa tshig gsal*. Dharamsala: Tibetan Publishing House, 1967. Partially translated by Theodore Stcherbatsky in *The Conception of Buddhist Nirvāṇa* and Mervyn Sprung in *Lucid Exposition of the Middle Way* (see below).

Chang, Garma C. C. *Six Yogas of Naropa & Teachings on Mahamudra*. Ithaca, NY: Snow Lion, 1977 (first edition 1963).

Ch'en, Kenneth. *Buddhism in China: A Historical Survey*. Princeton: Princeton University Press, 1964.

Cleary, Thomas and J. C. (trs.) *The Blue Cliff Record*. Boulder: Shambhala, 1977.

Conze, Edward. *Perfect Wisdom: The Short Prajñāpāramitā Texts*. Totnes: Buddhist Publishing Group, 1993 (first published 1973).

Dowman, Keith. *The Flight of the Garuda*. Boston: Wisdom, 1994.

—. *Masters of Mahamudra: Songs and Histories of the Eighty-four Buddhist Siddhas*. Albany: State University of New York Press, 1985.

Drew, John. *India and the Romantic Imagination*. Delhi: Oxford University Press, 1987.

Garfield, Jay L. *The Fundamental Wisdom of the Middle Way: Nāgārjuna's* Mūlamadhyamakākarikā. New York/Oxford: Oxford University Press, 1995.

Gendun Drup. *dBu ma rtsa ba shes rab kyi ngag don bshad pa rin po che'i phreng ba*. Sarnath: 1968.

Gittings, Robert (ed.). *Selected Poems and Letters of John Keats*. London: Heineman, 1966.

Gnoli, Raniero. *Nāgārjuna: Madhyamaka kārikā, Le stanze del cammino di mezzo*. Torino: 1961.

Hamilton, Sue. *Identity and Experience: The Constitution of the Human Being According to Early Buddhism*. London: Luzac Oriental, 1996.

Holmes, Richard. *Coleridge: Early Visions*. London: Hodder & Stoughton, 1989.

—. *Coleridge: Darker Reflections*. London: HarperCollins, 1998.

Hopkins, Jeffrey. *Meditation on Emptiness*. London: Wisdom Publications, 1983.

Huntington, C. W., Jr. *The Emptiness of Emptiness: An Introduction to Early Indian Mādhyamika*. Honolulu: University of Hawaii Press, 1989.

Inada, Kenneth K. *Nāgārjuna: A Translation of his* Mūlamadhyamakākarikā *with an Introductory Essay*. Tokyo: Hokuseido Press, 1970.

de Jong, J. W. *A Brief History of Buddhist Studies in Europe and America*. Delhi: Sri Satguru Publications, 1987.

Kalupahana, David J. *Nagarjuna: The Philosophy of the Middle Way*. Albany: State University of New York Press, 1986.

Kim, Hee-Jin. *Dōgen Kigen—Mystical Realist*. Tucson: University of Arizona Press, 1975.

Komito, David Ross. *Nāgārjuna's* "Seventy Stanzas": *A Buddhist Psychology of Emptiness*. Ithaca, NY: Snow Lion, 1987.

Lindtner, Chr. *Nagarjuniana: Studies in the Writings and Philosophy of Nāgārjuna*. Delhi: Motilal Banarsidass, 1987 (first published 1982).

Motion, Andrew. *Keats*. London: Faber, 1997.

Murti, T. R. V. *The Central Philosophy of Buddhism: A Study of the Mādhyamika System*. London: George Allen and Unwin, 1955.

Nāgārjuna. *Verses from the Center*. (*Mūlamadhyamakakārikā*). Tibetan: *dBu ma rtsa ba'i tshig le'ur byas pa shes rab ces bya ba*. (1) Tibetan text edited by Prof. L. P. Lhalungpa. Delhi: 1970. (2) Woodblock to Laser Source CD, Release A. Washington, D.C.: Asian Classics Input Project, 1993. Translated into English from Sanskrit by Kalupahana, Inada and Streng, and from Tibetan by Garfield (see above and below).

—. Tr. Lozang Jamspal, Ngawang Samten Chophel, Peter Della Santina. *Nāgārjuna's Letter to King Gautamīputra*. Delhi: Motilal Banarsidass, 1978.

—. Tr. John Dunne and Sara McClintock. *The Precious Garland: An Epistle to a King*. Boston: Wisdom Publications, 1997.

Ñāṇamoli, Bhikkhu. *The Life of the Buddha*. Kandy: Buddhist Publication Society, 1978.

Ñāṇananda, Bhikkhu. *Concept and Reality in Early Buddhist Thought*. Kandy: Buddhist Publication Society, 1971.

Obermiller, E. (tr.) *The History of Buddhism in India and Tibet by Bu-ston*. Delhi: Sri Satguru, 1986 (first published 1932).

Rabten, Geshe. Tr. Stephen Batchelor. *Echoes of Voidness*. London: Wisdom, 1983.

Ricard, Matthieu (tr.). *The Life of Shabkar: The Autobiography of a Tibetan Yogin*. Albany: State University of New York Press, 1994.

Robinson, Richard H. *Early Mādhyamika in India and China*. Delhi: Motilal Banarsidass, 1976 (first edition 1965).

Ruegg, David Seyfort. *The Literature of the Madhyamaka School of Philosophy in India*. Wiesbaden: Otto Harrassowitz, 1981.

Shabkar Tsoknyi Rangdrol. *'Od gsal rdzogs pa chen po'i khregs chod lta ba'i glu dbyangs sa lam ma lus myur du bgrod pa'i rtsal ldan mkha' lding gshog rlabs*. Tashijong Khampagar: nd. Translated by Keith Dowman as *The Flight of the Garuda* (see above).

—. *'Od gsal rdzogs pa chen po'i lhun grub thod rgal gyi glu dbyangs ting 'dzin sgo 'phar brgya phrag gcig car 'byed pa'i lde'u mig.* Tashijong Khampagar: nd.

Shāntideva. (1) Tr. Stephen Batchelor. *A Guide to the Bodhisattva's Way of Life.* Dharamsala: LTWA, 1979. (2) Tr. Kate Crosby and Andrew Skilton. *The Bodhicaryāvatāra.* Oxford: Oxford University Press, 1995.

Sprung, Mervyn. *Lucid Exposition of the Middle Way: The Essential Chapters from the* Prasannapadā *of Candrakīrti.* London: RKP, 1979.

Stcherbatsky, Theodore. *The Conception of Buddhist Nirvana.* Delhi: Motilal Banarsidass, 1977 (first edition 1927).

Streng, Frederick. *Emptiness—A Study in Religious Meaning.* Nashville, New York: Abingdon, 1967.

Tanahashi, Kazuaki (ed.). *Moon in a Dewdrop: Writings of Zen Master Dōgen.* Berkeley: North Point Press, 1985.

Thurman, Robert A. F. *Tsong Khapa's Speech of Gold in the* Essence of True Eloquence*: Reason and Enlightenment in the Central Philosophy of Tibet.* Princeton: Princeton University Press, 1984.

Tsongkhapa. *An Ocean of Reason: A Great Exposition of the Root Text Verses from the Center (rTsa she tik chen rigs pa'i rgya mtsho).* Varanasi: mTho slob dge ldan spyi las khang, 1973.

Tuck, Andrew P. *Comparative Philosophy and the Philosophy of Scholarship: On the Western Interpretation of Nāgārjuna.* New York: Oxford University Press, 1990.

Waley, Arthur (tr.). *The Way and Its Power: A Study of the Tao Te Ching and Its Place in Chinese Thought.* New York: Grove, 1958.

Walleser, M. *The Life of Nāgārjuna from Tibetan and Chinese Sources.* Delhi: Asian Educational Services, 1990.

Warder, A. K. *Indian Buddhism.* Delhi: Motilal Banarsidass, 1970.

Watson, Burton (tr.). *Chuang Tzu: Basic Writings.* New York: Columbia University Press, 1964.

Welbon, Guy Richard. *The Buddhist Nirvana and its Western Interpreters.* Chicago: University of Chicago Press, 1968.

Yamada, Koun. *Gateless Gate.* Los Angeles: Center Publications, 1979.

Yampolsky, Philip B. *The Platform Sutra of the Sixth Patriarch.* New York: Columbia University Press, 1967.

Yasutani, Hakuun. Tr. Paul Jaffe. *Flowers Fall: A Commentary on Zen Master Dōgen's* Genjōkōan. Boston: Shambhala, 1996.

Zurcher, E. *The Buddhist Conquest of China: The Spread and Adaptation of Buddhism in Early Medieval China.* Leiden: 1959.

About the Author

Stephen Batchelor is a former monk in the Tibetan and Zen traditions, and the author of the national best-seller *Buddhism Without Beliefs*. Batchelor's translations are known around the world as both definitive and beautifully composed. He has translated Shantideva's *A Guide to the Bodhisattva's Way of Life,* and written several books on Buddhism, including *Alone with Others, The Faith to Doubt, The Tibet Guide* (winner of the 1988 Thomas Cook Award), and *The Awakening of the West* (a joint winner of the 1994 Tricycle Award). He lectures and conducts meditation retreats worldwide, and is a contributing editor of *Tricycle,* a guiding teacher at Gaia House Retreat Centre, and director of studies at Sharpham College for Buddhist Studies and Contemporary Enquiry in Devon, England.

A Note on the Type

The text of this book is set in Perpetua. The display type is Metropolis Light. The book was designed by Chris Welch, and was printed and bound by R. R. Donnelley & Sons at Bloomsburg, Pennsylvania.